An Anatomy of Lying

An Anatomy of Lying

◆

In Personal Life and Society

Pujie Zheng

iUniverse, Inc.
New York Lincoln Shanghai

An Anatomy of Lying
In Personal Life and Society

iUniverse books may be ordered through booksellers or by contacting:

iUniverse
2021 Pine Lake Road, Suite 100
Lincoln, NE 68512
www.iuniverse.com
1-800-Authors (1-800-288-4677)

Author's Photo by Wei Zheng

ISBN-13: 978-0-595-38602-4 (pbk)
ISBN-13: 978-0-595-82983-5 (ebk)
ISBN-10: 0-595-38602-4 (pbk)
ISBN-10: 0-595-82983-X (ebk)

Printed in the United States of America

To My Parents

Zheng Shaotang and Wang Rulin

Contents

Introduction

○ ○

Lie loses souls,
Death loses body.

—St. Augustine[1]

At the beginning of my career, as a student of engineering and science, life was easy as things were judged by simple rules: Any engineering design, if not working, is worthless; and any scientific theory, if conflicting with the real world phenomena, is wrong.

As life progressed and I began to work in the private sector managing software development projects, the line started blurring, just like what Dante said in his *Inferno*,

> Midway upon the journey of our life
> I found myself within a forest dark,
> For the straightforward pathway had been lost.[2]

Increasingly, I had to deal with people and the issue of lying. The investigation into the matter amazed me so much that I ended up putting my notes together in the form of a book. Two years after the work was done, additional experience made the issue even more amazing. In the grand scheme of things, the study gave me a clearer picture of people and the world.

Before coming to the U.S. from China in 1985, I lived in a country where the government had absolute control of the information that its citizens may access. Its manipulative skills were such that it could, for its own political purposes, use factual information effectively to fan the emotions of the Chinese people, young and old, well-educated as well as uneducated. The Great Proletarian Cultural

---

1. St. Augustine: *On lying*
2. Dante Alighieri: *The Divine Comedy*, translated by Henry Wadsworth Longfellow

Revolution from 1966 to 1976 was the highlight of such success when the Chinese people passionately persecuted one another before they themselves were made victims. The ten-year madness ruined a generation. Subsequent Chinese regimes, from Deng Xiaoping, to Jiang Zemin, to Hu Jintao who is in power today, have forbidden any independent study of the episode because they employ much of the practice that Mao Zedong used in the Cultural Revolution.

Many Chinese people, although a small minority, understand the hideous nature of such practice, but they choose to remain silent nonetheless because they do not want to spend the rest of their lives in jail. Many of them find sanctuaries in scientific research institutions where the lines of right and wrong are clear. As a college undergraduate student of electrical engineering at Qinghua University, which has consistently been ranked the best university in China, I spent little time thinking outside of the confines of mathematics, physics, and electrical engineering.

With a fellowship[3] from the University of Virginia, I came to the U.S. as a graduate student to study physics. At first, I thought that I had successfully exited the shadow of lies, as I was impressed by the universality of the U.S. universities that were willing to give learning opportunities to anyone worldwide. But I soon found out that it was nothing but a financial scheme for universities to circumvent minimum wage laws. Under the banner of "graduate study", universities hired graduate students typically into PhD programs below the minimum wages to conduct research and hands-on teaching, so professors could concentrate on attracting research funding. The money-attracting ability determines professors' importance in universities, instead of the ability to educate youngsters. Facing that reality, there were not enough American undergraduate students willing to enter these programs, forcing universities to turn abroad and fill the graduate schools with foreign students.

I taught undergraduate students and conducted research under a person who called himself my mentor for five years before I was hit by the second big lie in my life. The lie came in several strikes. The first was the cutting of the research funding. The second strike came when the university refused to provide assistance for me to finish the PhD project[4]. The third strike came when my mentor asked me to find a new mentor and a new project. It was a puzzling phenomenon that this situation happened to the Chinese students more as a rule than an

---

3.   It included living stipends and a waiver of tuitions and fees.
4.   When my mentor applied for the same assistance for his next student, who happened to be a white American, he got the money and the student duly got his PhD degree.

exception, but not to the American students. When other Chinese students ran into similar situations, they always "chose" another mentor. In five years, as if by miracles, they would not run into the same situation again and get their PhD degree. After I told him that I'd like to leave with a master's degree, my "mentor" for five years who had repeatedly told me that I had done enough work to be worthy of a *PhD* degree wrote me a note saying that he could not, out of his conscience, give me a *master's* degree because I did not deserve it, after working for him for five years.

For those who are not familiar with the academic field, I need to make a note here that the situation has improved a great deal after several professors were murdered by their graduate students under similar situations. After hearing the first case, which was a Chinese student murdering his mentor who happened to be white[5], I remember talking with some students regretting the stupid decision of the young student, throwing his life away (the student shot himself immediately after killing his professor and several other innocent people) in exchange of a worthless old man. "I am sorry," the wife of a graduate student cut into the conversation, "but I feel good. More of these people should be killed." I have to confess that, although my mind was not with her, my heart certainly was.

At the University of Virginia, I came to know Thomas Jefferson. It amazed me that, in the country that was established according to his plan and still revering his masterful thinking, the undertaking to correct the abuse of graduate students took the form of multiple murders. If I understand Jefferson correctly, he probably would have considered these murderers as unfortunate martyrs who corrected a practice that had wronged them. At the same time, he would turn in his tomb that such wrongs could not be righted in a more civilized manner in his country. Alas, it must be a healthy thing to have minor revolutions here and there.

As Mao Zedong has said that "no revolution is a dinner party," a few bad apples among the vast number of abusive professors received the capital punishment that is, unquestionably, too harsh for them. Even abusive professors do not deserve that, but the Chinese students have no way to fight back except by extreme measures.

Take my own experience for example. When I was about to leave the University of Virginia in 1990 (without a master's degree after working there for a PhD degree for five years), my "mentor" told me that, without his recommendation, I could never find a job in "his" country. Without a job, I would be forced to go

---

5.   There have been subsequent cases including a white student murdering an ethnic Chinese professor.

back to China. He made such comment to me in 1990 with full knowledge that I was involved in the student movement. After lobbying the U.S. Congress to extend permanent resident status to all Chinese nationals, coordinating demonstrations against the Chinese government that rolled tanks into Tiananmen Square to suppress the student movement, and arranging activities of the escaped student leaders on their first trip to Washington, DC, my name was out there. One has to be personally in one of these situations to understand the hideous and savaging nature of these professors.

A powerful friend of mine made a threat to my "mentor" that if he refused to grant me the master degree, my friend would see to it that my "mentor" would never get a penny from the federal government. Grudgingly, my mentor changed his mind and agreed that I deserved a master's degree. The degree came three years later.

That was one of the lowest points of my life. After China, I had lived at the University of Virginia under the shadow of lies for five years. The fact that I did not recognize the lie at the beginning made the experience so much more painful.

Devastated, I aimlessly landed a job in Fujifilm's medical division in the U.S. , and started my recovery. Certainly, I had to deal with bureaucratic problems, but largely, I was allowed to use my skill to serve the customers. My career developed in the direction of technical and corporate management. Once I started managing people, the issue of lying came back to me as I had to deal with excuses, bureaucratic maneuvers, conspiracies, and outright incompetence.

Although the world has been progressing consistently and becoming a more reasonable place, the bureaucratic undercurrent is still strong, constantly pushing companies in the direction of false sense of security and incompetence. Leaders have to swim hard against the trend to make the company cultures moving in the direction of truth and merit.

Today, even after the global change of environment since the 1980s, the majority of the American business managers still could not measure up to the basic standard[6]. Many current movements to deal with the problems miss the mark. For instance, in response to the problems that companies could not effectively manage projects, Project Management Institute starts to license Project Management Professionals. These professionals present themselves as jack-of-all-trade project managers holding the solution to all project management problems and openly claim that companies should not allow technologists (i.e., people who understand the business itself) to manage projects. Several decades earlier, com-

---

6.   See Chapter 6

panies went through one of these follies by blindly taking Masters of Business Administration who also did not understand the businesses as the solution of corporate profitability. As skunk works had demonstrated in the 1960s, PMPs, like MBAs, are no substitute for understanding of the business and people involved. It is fascinating that businesses flock itself toward such "solutions" that do not even address the problems in theory. Any competent corporate executive would have stood up and asked: What part of the certification process assures that these PMPs are good leaders.

Different people are under the shadow of different lies. Once, an acquaintance of mine nonchalantly told me that using drug was no big deal. Who was she kidding as she spoke under the specter of the chemicals, not to mention the risk of running afoul with the criminal justice system?

Many people believe that they would be happy if they have more money at their disposal, but seeing those super rich Chinese business people gambling away their money in Las Vegas, I do not sense much happiness. Living in what is becoming an ethnic Chinese community in Arcadia, a Los Angeles suburb, I know for a fact that most of them are not happy.

Recently, a friend of mine from China insisted that China was a free country after staying in the U.S. for six months. Certainly, China has become freer, but it is nowhere near the international standard of a free country. The friend closed his mind when I suggested him to ask political dissidents or *Falun Gong*[7] practitioners in Chinese jails.

In the U.S., politicians travel around the country in election seasons to persuade voters that the U.S. is the best and freest country in the world. The underlying message, of course, is that the people should be complacently happy about what they already have and demand less from the politicians, while the reality is that, in a shrinking world where competition is becoming increasingly fierce, complacency is the last thing that the country needs.

In a grander scale, most of us believe that human beings are secure and powerful, but that ignores our vulnerability and that of the earth. For instance, few people are even aware of the possibility that a supernova explosion nearby would wipe us out with absolutely no forewarning because the radioactive shockwave would come at the speed of light. Besides knowing that a few stars are at the state

---

7.   Started as a *qigong* (Chinese breathing meditation) practice, *Falun Gong* has evolved into a full-fledged religion, although some practitioners deny it. Further readings of *Falun Gong* can be found in books written by its founder, Li Hongzhi.

to explode, we have no clue how to forecast, let alone how to deal with, such an event. In fact, human beings cannot even predict earth's weather accurately.

In every decision we make and every action we take, there is an issue of truthfulness. In fact, intentional misrepresentation is only a small part of falsehood. We subconsciously lie to ourselves and others constantly; organizations deceive their members sometimes indiscernibly but always powerfully; even logic, such as Prisoner's Dilemma[8], works against us by forcing us to lie. From a semi-abstract level, we are brainwashed to believe the greatness of the public educational system while agreeing that it discharges its responsibilities poorly; we believe that the American business system is the most effective in the world while seeing that incompetent managers run organizations and competent managers could not find jobs; and we believe in different and often conflicting explanations of our economic problems that different politicians provide us, while knowing that the politicians are spinning the issue for the interests of themselves and the special interest groups that support them financially.

This book is a personal journey to sort out those issues.

Chapter 1 goes through several related concepts, such as belief, logic, fact, understanding, and abstraction, before defining truth.

Chapter 2 covers different processes that our bodies use to handle problems (e.g., hormonal process, subconscious filters, habit, etc.) and discusses the courage needed to seek truth.

Chapter 3 discusses lies that we bestow to one another.

Chapter 4 considers organizations as individual entities and discusses their psychological behaviors, inwardly and outwardly.

After Chapter 1 through 4 lay the foundations, Chapters 5 through 9 go over different social systems.

Chapter 5 considers education and the educational system, the key of producing a truthful, happy, wise, and confident child, and the difficulties of accomplishing that with a double third-party payer system that isolates service receivers (i.e., students) and service providers (i.e., teachers).

Chapter 6 discusses the business system and the issues of corporate management, corporate malfeasance, and corporate finance.

Chapter 7 covers the economic system. First from mercantilism to Keynesianism, and recently from Keynesianism to free market, the changes represent the hope of the world in its brutal approach toward truth, understanding, and pro-

---

8.   See Chapter 3

ductivity. The economic power spreads democracy, with a few exceptions, throughout the world. This revolution, which has been largely bloodless, has come to the point that puts the U.S. at test to see whether it could keep its global economic leading position.

Chapter 8 is on the political system—discussing political deceptions in informational (e.g., tax reporting) and non-informational (e.g., border patrol) processes.

Chapter 9 discusses international relations.

Chapter 10, the concluding chapter, discusses the nature's games and ways to keep the human progress going.

I would like to thank my parents who discussed the topic with me from their perspectives when I started putting my notes together four years ago. I would also like to thank Wei who was a constant source of encouragement to me when the lion share of the work was done two years ago. Now, as my wife, she pushed me to put the book together and publish it.

Pujie Zheng
Arcadia
January 2006

1

Defining Truth and Deception

o o o o o o o o o o o o o o o o o o o o o o o o o o o o o o o o o

Dao[1] gives birth to one;
One gives birth to two;
Two gives birth to three;
Three gives birth to everything in the world.

—*Lao Zi*[2]

The definition of truth is tricky. Some define it as anything factual, which is an oversimplification in today's world because that definition considers the Washingtonian sport of spinning as telling truth. Others define it as the result of empirical investigations of usefulness or practicality. Any sales professional would say that the reverse is true—almost all useful sales tricks are deceptive. Those who define truth as experts' agreement also have troubles. For instance, for much of the 20th century, the overwhelming majority of economists, as well as the public, agreed that the Keynesian theories of powerful government and vigorous intervention were the keys to economic success. To them, there was no doubt that the Keynesian theories were correct. At the height of Keynesianism's popularity, Friedrich von Hayek, a free-market economist, joked that he was the only person in the world believing in free market. When Margaret Thatcher started her reforms with the support of a handful of economists, 364 others wrote to *The Times* (London) claiming that she was wrong. The majority of economists finally changed their minds, not by their analytical work but by the accomplishments of political practitioners such as Thatcher in Britain, Ronald Reagan in the U.S. , and Deng Xiaoping in China. That definition also flies in the face of evidence

---

1. *Dao* (Chinese: 道) is also translated as *Tao*.
2. Lao Zi: *Dao De Jing*, author's translation.

that in scientific development, truth in the beginning has always been in the hands of a few.

According to Merriam-Webster Online[3], truth is defined as the collection of the following:

1. the state of being the case

2. the body of real things, events, and facts

3. a transcendent fundamental or spiritual reality

4. a judgment, proposition, or idea that is true or accepted as true

5. the body of true statements and propositions

6. the property (as of a statement) of being in accord with fact or reality

7. fidelity to an original or to a standard

From those definitions, we can get a rough idea about the word but could not use them to determine truth, because they are composed of oversimplifications, circular logic, or dependent concepts (i.e., "the case", "real", "reality", "true", "fact", "original", and "standard").

To Plato, truth equaled to good and reality. Then, Friedrich Nietzsche claimed that the world was beyond good and evil. Things got so confused that Donald Davidson, an American philosopher, finally declared "The Folly of Trying to Define Truth".[4]

Before we set out on our journey, we need a better definition of truth.

Often, beliefs are confused with truth. When people fail to find truth, they settle for beliefs, which may or may not be the same thing. Religions throughout the world get their popularity by answering commonly held questions, such as those concerning creation, birth, the meaning of life, and death, using hypothesis and interlocking logic.

American religious organizations are quite successful with the Chinese students in the U.S. because they fill a void. In China, children are brainwashed by the Chinese Communist Party and are not allowed to think outside of the Party-defined boundaries. When they come to the U.S. , the pressure from the Communist Party is gone, leaving them with a spiritual void. Too busy making a living in the U.S., they have no time to explore the grand scheme of things

3.   http://www.m-w.com (11/26/2002)
4.   *Journal of Philosophy*, 1996, pp. 263-279

themselves. Churches fill the void. Indirectly, this proves that "graduate student" is a disguised job title, for if graduate students are real students, they should be allowed time to explore.

Generations of religious thinkers have worked on the consistency of different beliefs to form coherent bodies of theories, while scientists have taken another approach by starting with the simplest mechanical phenomena and using mathematics to derive theories that expand the human understanding into gravity, electricity, molecules, atoms, etc. The two groups of thinkers collided until Voltaire came to the scene to elucidate the differences. He did such a good job that few people still read his arguments today, since he had settled that scores once and for all.

Although beliefs are true to the believers, they are not the truth.

For one group of people, belief comes close to truth, because loosely speaking, they believe in truth[5]. Frank Lloyd Wright advanced the concept when he said that his God was Nature with a capital "N". We can find that trace in many creative thinkers, such as Nicolaus Copernicus, Galileo, and Albert Einstein. The trouble is that one could not put his finger on Wright's Nature as easy as he could on quantum mechanics.

Logic is not truth either. Take economy for example. It is easy for anyone to read books on economics (i.e., the rules) and be fluent with the theories, but understanding an economy (i.e., the reality), such as the U.S. economy, is an entirely different affair. The difference is that we have thousands of excellent economists but only a few (e.g., Alan Greenspan) truly understand the U.S. economy.

Good theories could be used to reach false conclusions often just as easily as bad theories. The garbage-in-garbage-out process could cause that to happen. For instance, it does not matter how good an investment theory is. When it is based on false information, the investor should expect to lose.

Facts are not truth. The Chinese government is good at using facts to spread falsehood about the U.S. . When the U.S. government tried to force the Chinese government to stop exporting products made by prison labor, I was in China and watched that the Chinese television (1) reported the American side of the news exactly the way it was reported in the U.S. , (2) stated the Party policy that the

---

5.   Excuse me here for being out of order with the circular logic, as "truth" has not yet been defined.

Chinese government did not export prisoner-made goods abroad, (3) displayed brochures of American prisons advertising their prisoner-made products to potential Chinese customers, and (4) ran special reports on American prisons' poor performance of reforming criminals.

When the American government pushed for China to stop the one-child policy, the Chinese government went around calculating the outcome of uncontrolled population explosion. The numbers were so shocking that any Chinese with elementary school math could understand the government's point—the United States wanted to use uncontrolled population growth to destroy China.

When it came to the stories of U.S. spy planes flying over Chinese waters (according to the Chinese definition), or the U.S. bombing of the Chinese Embassy in Belgrade in 1999, the Chinese government did not have to spin much. The reports clearly made the Chinese people think that the U.S. was the enemy of China. Many Chinese believe that the U.S. government has an ongoing policy to damage China. They simply laughed at me when I suggested that it was a CIA screw-up.

Such manipulations—by using facts to spread falsehood—have been quite influential. When terrorists attacked the U.S. on September 11, 2001, students of Beijing University, for instance, burst into spontaneously celebration throughout the campus. The senseless murdering of innocent civilians of so many nations, including China, did not seem to register in their minds. The government propaganda blinded them, as they wanted to see Americans hurt, no matter how, proving an age-old truth: angry fools are the most dangerous people. Under the Communist propaganda, the students of Beijing University joined that sad club. (The interesting thing is that, upon graduation, they would line up in front of the U.S. Consulates applying for visas to come to the U.S.)

In fact, fictions are often an outstanding vehicle to convey truth. Works of William Shakespeare, Charles Dickens, Leo Tolstoy, Victor Hugo, and Dante Alighieri are timeless because they elucidate truth that transcends era and culture. In fact, when fictional work tells truth, it does not have to achieve high degree of literary artistry to survive. Ayn Rand's *The Fountainhead*, a somewhat awkward philosophical novel, has remained in print since the Bobbs-Merrill Company first published it in 1943.

Today, with cutthroat competition in publishing business, many bestselling novels fit better on the magazine racks because of their short lifespan, caused by the authors' effort to jerk the emotions of the readers, rather than tell the truth.

In painting, Pablo Picasso certainly shakes the author; Andy Warhol amuses me; and Claude Monet gives me the poetic pleasure of tranquility. But I have to admit that I still don't understand much of the modern paintings—a yellow circle on uneven orange pigment strikes me as decorative at best. Many pieces in museums give me the sense of vulgar. Profound ugliness reveals truth in life, which is undoubtedly art, but displaying a urinal at a different angle and explaining that as viewing life from another perspective are acts of dried-up inspirations on the part of the artist as well as the critic. In a way, truth and humanity are expressed in paintings just as they are expressed in novels. Ah Chong[6], a Hong Kong artist who paints mostly worms these days, told me that he changed his name to Ah Chong after working for newspapers for over two decades, because he wanted to draw a world of love and harmony rather than hostility. All lasting art works reveal profound truth. Similarly, when music is developed into nothing but loud beats for physical stimulation, it becomes noise without art—a sort of sex without love.

Art (e.g., novels, paintings, and music) is a vehicle. The vehicle itself, which is the art form, is certainly important. But to evaluate work of art, one has to weigh the content first and foremost. Ah Chong said that as he focused his attention on the emotions of the Hong Kong people, the art form, which was the traditional Chinese ink painting on rice paper with an abstractive twist, came to him naturally. The longevity of *The Fountainhead* over many better-written novels also illustrates this point. I am not a fan of rap music, but when Shakespeare is read in rap, the anger expressed in it reveals the true human nature. When rap is used to carry anger with nothing but profanity, it conveys just vulgar.

Understanding truth is not an easy matter, as Louis Armstrong once said, "Unless you know what it is, I ain't never going to be able to explain it to you."[7] Armstrong was not even talking about composing jazz, but about the ability to understand and enjoy the pieces passively.

The lack of understanding leads to false beliefs. When people act upon those false beliefs, falsities are the natural outcome. Once, a Chinese friend of mine visited me from Canada. Over dinner, he told me that English poems were no comparison to Chinese poems.

"What do you think about Shakespeare?" I asked.

---

6. "Ah Chong" literally means "Lovely Worm" in Chinese. His legal name is Yan Yijing.

7. Anthony Smith: *The Mind,* The Viking Press, p. 146 (1987)

"That is what I am talking about," he replied. "His poems are no comparison to Li Bai's[8]."

"Does Shakespeare move you at all? Does he give you any strong emotions?"

"No," answered the PhD friend of mine.

I did not know what to say for a while. Then, I went ahead to offend him by suggesting that he might not understand English poems.

It is sad to imagine how many students are out there passing poetry classes by using their memory skills instead of their power of understanding. It makes me think about the movie *Dead Poet Society*[9] and the scarcity of the likes of Mr. Keating who explains poems to his students. It is sadder to consider that the educational system has a strong tendency to squeeze these true teachers out of the system[10].

Understanding leads to abstractions. For instance, "all men are dogs" is an abstraction about men. Keynesianism is an abstraction of economics and governmental economic policies.

Different abstractions have different degrees. For instance, the government policy on poverty (e.g., the belief that providing food and shelter to the poor would solve the poverty problems) has a lower degree of abstraction than the general economic policy (e.g., Keynesianism). Higher degree abstractions are more powerful than lower degree ones.

When abstractions are accepted as truth, they quickly become instinct—the ability for us to make decisions without thinking[11].

Unfortunately, no abstraction is true absolutely. The abstraction "all men are dogs" could be true with a limited collection of men. Some might argue that Keynesianism is true at the first stage of implementation before reaching stagflation, while others think that it is never true.

At times, theories with wider areas of applicability (i.e., higher degree of abstraction) might not be convenient to use in specific situations. For instance, one might say that Newton's view of the world is less true than Einstein's, but when we calculate for the best way to lift a heavy object, such as an oil refinery tower, Newton's theories would work out much better. In fact, specific formulas have been developed to simplify the calculations even further.

---

8.   Li Bai, a Chinese poet of the *Tang* dynasty (618–907), is also translated as Li Po

9.   *Dead Poets Society,* Touchstone Pictures, 1989

10.   See Chapter 5.

11.   See discussions about subconscious filter in Chapter 2.

Higher degree abstractions, when true, always bring us more power. In American government, the highest form of abstraction is stated in Jefferson's *Declaration of Independence* and the Bill of Rights. All other measures, such as the formation of government, the economic policies, or racial policies, are of lower degrees. Those who understand higher-degree abstractions are better equipped to handle lower-degree problems. For instance, Abraham Lincoln was one of the best students of Jefferson. If he had been allowed to operate for a term or two in the White House after the Civil War, the subsequent U.S. history on race would have been entirely different, because he would have undoubtedly used the short period of extraordinary politics when the euphoric public would have given him a great deal of latitude to implement reconciliatory policies. In fact, before his assassination, Lincoln had already shown his masterful hands of reconciliation.

Andrew Johnson, Lincoln's successor, "was one of the most unfortunate of Presidents," according to the White House[12]. The misfortune was in fact America's. On one hand, Johnson allowed the southern states to apply the so-called "black codes" to discriminate the former slaves. On the other hand, he failed to handle the northern radicals, who, after pushing him for a multitude of uncompromising measures, moved to impeach him, and failed by only one vote in the Senate.

Differences in the comprehension of abstractions created the sharp contrast between Lincoln and Johnson. That comprehension, in operating an organization, is known as "the vision thing". Since Johnson did not have a vision, he merely reacted in the White House, missing precious opportunities to resolve racial problems.

When we are young, we strive to achieve excellence, which is the mastering of abstractions in specific areas. Many of us manage to achieve that. After going through several areas and accomplishing excellence, we come across a critical point in life. At that point, it takes enormous courage to do what Robert Frost suggested:

> Two roads diverged in a wood, and I—
> I took the one less traveled by,
> And that has made all the difference.[13]

---

12. http://www.whitehouse.gov/history/presidents/aj17.html (12/5/2002)
13. From Robert Frost's *Mountain Interval*

That is time for maturity, which is a higher level of abstraction than excellence in a limited field or several isolated fields. The move from excellence to maturity is not a quantitative improvement, but a qualitative jump because in maturity we know the inner connections of things, allowing us to understand the abstraction of other fields of human knowledge without the underlying details. It takes a long time for anyone to get to that beautiful state because there is no shortcut, but once there, we get many wonderful byproducts, such as confidence, comfort with ourselves and the world around us, and peace of mind.

We may also view excellence and maturity from another angle. All empires start with excellence, often military excellence. As the expansion reaches its technical, economic, military, or cultural limit, the durability of the empire depends on its maturity—the ability of the top leaders to comprehend new situations and make wise decisions to allow every kind of excellence from both inside and outside to succeed and be integrated into the culture. The lack of maturity, which often takes the form of suppressing different ideas, puts the empire on a timer, waiting for the next excellence from either within or outside to destroy it. In that sense, the Chinese Empire formed more than 2,000 years ago has a higher degree of maturity than the Roman Empire.

One might say that maturity and excellence are merely different levels of abstraction to reflect reality.

After those discussions, the definition of truth becomes obvious: truth is the ultimate and correct abstraction that covers everything, a.k.a. *Dao*. Many people have spent their whole lives trying to push human understanding one-step closer to truth. For instance, Einstein, after the development of Special and General Relativity, went to work on his Unified Field Theory[14]. We human beings as a whole have been striving to obtain higher degree abstractions consciously which is how we distinguished ourselves in the animal kingdom. So far, the absolute truth (i.e., *Dao*) is nowhere in sight.

In the absence of absolute truth, all abstractions have their limitations, thus applicability. Unless the abstraction is wrong like Keynesianism, higher degree

---

14. Unified Field Theory is a single theory that explains four basic types of field—gravitational field, electromagnetic field, the weak field and the strong field. The weak and strong fields create the force that binds nuclei together. Einstein failed to discover the theory. Neither did anyone after him so far. But the beauty of the universe still makes many people, including the author, to believe that such a theory exists. Our level of abstraction, which limits our ability of comprehension, prevents us from seeing it.

abstractions carry fewer limitations and are applicable in more situations. In the recent 5,000 years, nations rise and fall according to their comprehension of abstractions and their creative abilities to take advantage of such comprehension. Up until 722 B.C., China had been a collection of small states under nominal emperors for some 2,000 years. For the next 500 years[15], with the emperor removed, kings of those states consciously focused their efforts on the development of abstractions to allow them to govern bigger areas. As abstractions advanced, the areas of states expanded. A magnificent set of abstractions ranging from political, military, economic, agricultural, to cultural was developed in that period. Finally, political reforms adopted by Ying Zheng gave his state, Qin, the final empowerment to conquer others. Although Ying Zheng's brutal and lavish Qin dynasty was quickly overthrown, future rulers have been using and perfecting his governing theories until today. The traditional political instinct is so deep-rooted in China that it has managed to ignore 500 years of Western scientific and democratic development. The modern concept of democracy, for instance, is still having trouble to enter China at the beginning of the 21st century. For instance, many successful Chinese business people have argued that Western democracy would only create chaos for China and should be avoided.

The paths to abstractions are always difficult and laborious. The American educational system has been teaching clichés by asking students to remember sporadic facts to pass tests rather than bringing students actual comprehensions of underlying abstractions. In a sense, the educational system carries out the task of making students to memorize tidbits about jazz without understanding the music. When I taught physics at the University of Virginia as a graduate student, it was clear that only a few percent of students cared about learning the subject. The overwhelming majority simply tagged along and, after going through the required motions, got a sheet of paper in the end.

Relatively speaking, the educational system is more successful in teaching simple abstract fields like mathematics than in compound fields like sociology. In mathematics, students could work on the real mathematical problems and gain comprehension of the underlying abstractions. In sociology, since the students have no way to practice different theories in the classrooms, they are merely indoctrinated or brainwashed by professors who often hold fundamentally different opinions from the general population. The college education of sociology is like learning oil painting without ever touching oil, or learning swimming with-

---

15.   The *Chunqiu* and *zhanguo* periods lasted from 722 B.C. to 221 B.C.

out ever touching water. The belief is based on nothing but professor's say-so. Since it is easier for students to get good grades by agreeing with the professors, modern education to most students is an indoctrination process instead of a learning process.

Human beings accomplish complex tasks by the application of technologies. For instance, a person who has never heard of Fast Fourier Transforms—a mathematical process that is responsible for turning multiple projections into tomography—could operate CT[16] machines. A person who has never heard of nuclear physics could operate machines to take MRI[17] images of a patient. Although hopeless in teaching abstractions, schools are typically good at teaching students the skills to operate such machines. The most important reason is that the teachers typically know how to operate those machines but do not understand the abstractions themselves.

The development of technologies produces two classes of people—those who produce technologies and those who use them. In the future, those who create technologies would command high remunerations and those who use them would be paid poorly because their jobs would become increasingly more replaceable with the deployment of new technologies. Members of the creative group would be paid highly because they must comprehend abstractions and figure out ways for people without the apprehension of the abstractions to use them. Unfortunately, even good engineering schools, which could provide their students with a view of the existing technologies, are utterly inept in teaching creativity and abstractions.

One area that technologies have failed to automate is management. Competent managers inspire innovative spirit (i.e., élan) and confidence in their employees. But these qualified managers, just like good teachers, are hard to come by. The majority of managers understand neither the issues that they are dealing with nor the abilities of their subordinates.

---

16. Computed Tomography uses a turning x-ray machine to obtain projections of a cross section of our body from different angles. Then, mathematical processes including the Fast Fourier Transforms produce images of that cross section.

17. Magnetic Resonance Imaging is an application of nuclear magnetic resonance to produce cross-sectional images of the bodies. Marketing people did not like the word "nuclear" so they cut the word out of the name. From scientific standpoint, the phrase "magnetic resonance" is absurd.

One interesting point that deserves notion here is the difference between lies (i.e., untrue or inaccurate statements that may or may not be believed by the speaker[18]) and unproven creative thoughts. "Create" is defined as "to bring into existence"[19]. The first step of obtaining abstraction is to make hypotheses or guesses. The second step is to find out whether the hypotheses are true. Without the help of abstractions, one has to use the simple method of elimination, which is a wasteful, and often impossible, undertaking of going through all possibilities. Drug companies today largely use that method to look for new drugs, which is partially responsible for the high prices of new drugs. Abstractions are obtained as effectively by recognizing falsity as by recognizing truth. The human experience of consciously seeking abstractions has not been smooth sailing, as we have often believed in false abstractions. For example, in the past 100 years, the entire human race first accepted the brilliant—but false—theories of Marxism-Keynesianism in the so-called capitalist nations and Marxism-Leninism in the so-called communist nations. The two groups even fought against each other and found decades later that they were both wrong, although the West claimed victory by giving up Marxism-Keynesianism first and then crushing the Marxist-Leninist camp with its economic power. One significant distinction between the East and the West is that the Western governments were democratic, while the Eastern governments were oligarchic and often geriatric.

Human beings beat the natural selection process with the efforts of consciously seeking abstractions (i.e., truth), which has distinguished us from our fellow animals, but as we shall see in the next chapter, they also bring us problems.

---

18. http://www.m-w.com/cgi-bin/dictionary (8/13/2002)
19. ibid.

2

The Personal Aspect

Man prefers to believe what he prefers to be true.

—Francis Bacon

Darwinian natural selection, through trial and error, sets up a biological process that equips us physically to hunt by instinct, but our ancestors outsmarted the biological system by seeking abstractions consciously, which in turn fueled the creative process to develop technological applications. One of their first accomplishments was to replace hunting with farming and husbandry, giving human beings a tremendous competitive advantage over other animals. With that advantage, human beings were able to spend more time comprehending abstractions and developing applications, usually by those who had passed childbearing age. Such development gradually became the main drive for human progress, outside of the natural selection process. The result is that our bodies stayed in the hunter's mode specializing in handling short-term crisis, by the so-called "fight or flight" process, while our society has moved on and rendered that mechanism useless and often counterproductive.

When receiving a stimulation (e.g., a threat), the brain sends signal to hypothalamus to secret CRF[1], which triggers the pituitary gland to release ACTH[2], opioids (e.g., endorphin), etc. These powerful chemicals allow us to gain instant heightened alert, attention, calm, tranquility, and clarity in mind. Under their influence, heart beats faster and blood pressure rises, putting all organs on overdrive. Brain stops reporting pain and forgets everything else to focus solely on the threat. In the hunting days, under the attack by a stronger animal, this height-

---

1.   Corticotropin-releasing factor
2.   Adrenocorticotrophic hormone

ened biochemical and biological state made us stronger than we really were and helped us make better decisions with the super concentration. In those days, the threat normally subsided in a short time so the body could return to its normal state.

Nature designed that biochemical process to handle only short and infrequent periods of threat. If the threat is persistent, the process becomes counterproductive. First, persistent opioid hits reduce the efficiency of the chemical, causing the body to demand more. When the opioid-producing mechanism reaches its maximum capacity, we would suffer from the ever-diminishing effect. Second, opioids are addictive. When the addiction, or reliance, is in place, even without external stimulation, the body craves for opioids. The delicate chemical balance of the body is therefore broken.

Today, we face mostly persistent-type stimuli, such as receiving low grades in school constantly or under the threat of losing jobs. What makes it worse is that many situations are beyond our control, such as the threat of job loss. Since our systems could not distinguish whether a threat is within or beyond our control, they simply presume that all threats are within our control and prepare the bodies for it, resulting in the problem that the bodies constantly receive signals to get excited, but none to relax, so we remain agitated, hostile, angry, cynical, and mentally preoccupied. After the bodies remain at the heightened alert state for too long, at some point, they would collapse, crashing into depression—a state of diminished interests and sadness, which is just as unpleasant as the aroused state.

Psychologically, post-traumatic stress disorders, emotional numbness, nervous irritability, depression, and sleeping difficulties are among the most common symptoms. Physiologically, gastrointestinal problems, respiratory disorders, skin disorders, hypertension, headaches, back pain, coronary heart disease, and cancer are common. Overall, the immune system is weakened, lowering our resistance to every disease.

One way to deal with the problem is by using narcotics, which is widely available and more accessible than alcohol and cigarettes to school-age children. In parties, people pass drugs around, knowing that by doing this together, they enhance one another's experience—a process known clinically as group therapy. When that practice becomes a part of culture, it is difficult for people, especially children, to resist. Many drug ingredients, such as THC[3], are hallucinogens,

---

3.   Tetrahydrocannabinol is a marijuana ingredient that gives out euphoric and tranquilizing effect.

making users appear dreamy, which is taken as cool by kids' culture. On the contrary, those who do not use drugs appear nerdy and outmoded.

The picture is not rosy in the other extreme, evidenced by the fact that most child geniuses fail to excel as adults. After meeting quite a few of them, I realize that stress is the most likely culprit. Receiving so many praises so early in their lives, they feel that they have an obligation to keep accomplishing impossible tasks to preserve their genius images, subjecting their tender bodies to unreasonable stress. They are forced to give up free spirit, independence, malcontent, and happiness. As grownups, they display no trace of leadership bones in them. Their strong self-discipline works against them as they remain in denial of their stress problems and suffer silently. Many modern-day academicians show similar psychological traits.

For adults, the situation is no better. Since the nature of the marketplace is uncertainty, those who carry profit and loss responsibilities, by definition, live unpredictable lives. That might be the reason that so few of us are entrepreneurs. When dockworkers of California, who earned six-figure income because of their monopoly, went on strike in 2002, many Californian importer-wholesalers were squeezed between the bad economy and the shipment delays, and found that they could not pass the increased cost, which amounted to 5-10% of the price, to their customers. Many importer-exporters, who were small and operated on entrepreneurial basis, had the doomsday threat hanging over their heads for months.

Many believe that they would experience less stress on salaried jobs. The problem of that theory is that, most people with salaried jobs leave their fate to managers who are, in general, notoriously ineffective to communicate bad news, so these people face the uncertainty beyond their control—the situation that our systems truly handle poorly.

Managers largely determine the mental states of the salaried employees. Once, GE ran into a technical problem with one of its big customers at the height of Jack Welch's tenure. After it was proven that the problem was at GE side, more and more GE bodies started to show up. Soon, there were some 20 GE guys including the regional manager on site. Finally, when they hit the jackpot, the right person solved the problem in 10 minutes. Under competent management, the onsite engineer should describe the problem to someone who could locate that right person. Under incompetent management, each one of those 20 GE employees went through unnecessary stress because they were sent to solve a problem that they could not. I had always wondered whether GE considered this a success under its six-sigma scheme, since the problem was solved timely.

Throwing bodies at problems *du jour* until they are solved is a sure sign of incompetent leaders. While putting unnecessary pressure on employees, it makes the entire organization behave neurotically and chaotically. After dealing with several organizations, I learned to assess the managers through organizational behaviors, which is probably the most reliable indicator of the competency of the managers, partly because most incompetent managers specialize in making impressive presentations to cover up their problems.

It is probably unfair to single out GE, arguably run by the best managers in the nation. I have seen many other companies, under similar situations, started to look for excuses and scapegoats. In fact, the majority of the managers that I had encountered simply do not understand the nature of the work that their subordinates are doing enough to make adequate evaluations of the quality and quantity of their work. When poor quality work causes problems at customer sites, they don't know how to solve them except by throwing bodies at the unfortunate customers, while running for cover themselves. GE's famed six-sigma methodology, in fact, is nothing more than a method to attach a number to such mishaps so managers could not hide them.

Incompetent managers believe that exerting additional pressures on subordinates always translate to higher productivity. Some do that consciously, and some unconsciously. To these managers, no amount of work is satisfactory. In other words, if subordinates finish a one-month assignment in a week, these incompetent managers would force them to do it in two days next time, thinking that they have not assigned enough work in the first place.

Over time, this tactic always backfires, especially in creative jobs, as it overloads productive employees to the point that they are miserable and have health problems, while other employees develop countermeasures. A friend of mine used to work for a software development company (what was known in the trade as an enterprise application integrator or EAI). Her bosses had no clue about the performances of employees. So everyone was compelled to "work" till 8 p.m. She told me once that if we needed to meet, the meeting had to be around 2 p.m. when she did her personal errands such as grocery shopping. Incidentally, the company put a lot of effort in different project management methodologies and produced almost every kind of charts. She remained miserable there for a year before finding another job.

I have always suspected that one of the reasons for the popularity of this management method is that it makes honest people miserable and thus less threatening to the incompetent managers, but a more likely explanation should be that the management simply load up the people who can solve the problems because they cannot make others productive. In such an environment, the incompetent would sharpen their self-protective skills with the management to protect their own turfs and interests. Honest and competent people have no chance to be happy there.

In American companies, only a small fraction of managers are competent enough to give clear instructions, lay out clear plans that do not require massive changes during execution, and formulate emergency response procedures that handle unexpected events successfully in an orderly manner without disrupting the normal functioning of the organizations. Under competent leadership, every member of the team uses the full extent of his or her creativity and individuality for the benefit of the customers. These managers do not typically invest a lot of their time producing impressive presentations and multitudes of charts. They would rather spend the time looking for potential problems, assessing risks, and developing solutions—functions that PMI[4] tries to de-emphasize.

So, we essentially face two options. One is to stand up against our wrongly designed body and take charge. The other is to allow the wrongly designed body to run our lives. The problem with the first option is that we have to be counter-intuitive all the time and always pick the road less traveled by—a habit not easy to keep. The problem with the second option is, of course, to allow the bad design to lead us to constant misery. It is always hard to use the first option and reject the second because it always seems easier to yield to self-deception by believing that there are no problems out there than figuring them out and solving them. It is too easy for us to believe that the company that we work for is the best company on the face of the earth; and our jobs are secure. It is so much easier to swallow the abuse of incompetent managers than to stand up against it. That is why company indoctrinations, even when they appear stupid to outsiders, work so well. Nature's faulty design of human beings has been frustrating us since we differentiate ourselves from animals. In China, 5,000 years ago, people used marijuana to relieve the stress.

Besides the faulty biological and psychological design, we have in us a powerful double edged sword, the so-called subconscious filters, to help reduce the workload of our conscious minds and make quicker decisions. The subconscious filters are a necessary part of our lives.

For example, I learned English as an adult. At the beginning, I consciously parsed the sentences to deduce their meanings, and often subsequently found

---

4.   Project Management Institute, see Introduction.

myself working on the inconsequential parts, therefore falling behind the speakers. (Children never comb sentences to apply grammatical analysis.) Later, as my English improved, the conscious mind worked less and less on parsing sentences, began to obtain the meaning automatically, and could anticipate speaker's key words. Finally, when I became fluent, I rarely paid attention to sentence structures. Only speaker's meanings reached my conscious mind, interacting nicely with my anticipations. I could almost say that I learned English by training my subconscious filters to process sentences automatically and send only the important meanings to the conscious mind. Since then, I sometimes had the reply ready before the speaker finished the sentence—a sort of overcharged anticipation.

The same process governs the learning of almost anything. For instance, when we start to play piano, we have to burden ourselves with all the details. Hitting the right combination of the keys in rapid succession according to some dots on paper is no small feat for the conscious mind. As we improve, the subconscious mind takes over, allowing the conscious mind to focus on music—expression and artistry. That is why professional piano players practice hours a day, everyday. They need their subconscious filters to be as finely tuned as possible.

That is also the reason that we measure a pilot's skill by the number of hours that he pilots the plane, but don't bother to ask whether those are good or bad hours. The supposition is that good hours and bad hours enhance the subconscious filters equally.

Such filtering also takes place in the cognitive field. When we meet people, our brains start to process the incoming information automatically. The subconscious filters process facial expressions, body languages, and spoken words. Men tend to ignore details such as what people wear, while women are more likely to remember those things partly because they consciously pay more attention to clothing in general. When women question men about clothing details, they are playing a little game with the mind, because the subconscious filters of caring men might filter out the clothing details.

In the U.S. , racial relation has always been a hot issue. Almost everyone agrees that achieving a race-ignorant society is the ultimate goal, under which our subconscious filters would take out the racial attributes. But that is not easy. When Shaq O'Neal was playing for the Los Angeles Lakers, I listened to him on television once, not conscious that he was black. As Shaq started talking about Jesse Jackson, instead of Phil Jackson, I suddenly became conscious that he was black, belonging to a different race. Coming to that realization, I felt a valley between Shaq and me, which was not there before.

Also, when Jesse Jackson hanged around Michael Jackson during Michael Jackson's trial in 2005, the fact that Michael Jackson was black came to my consciousness.

A few years ago, at a business dinner, one person started to tell racial jokes with the "N" word in almost every other sentence. He went on for a while until seeing me, and stopped in mid-sentence, not knowing how to take the situation.

The American culture is undoubtedly racially conscious, although everyone knows that the very consciousness is poisonous. The situation is not likely to change before the underlying differences between races are eliminated.

The Chinese government is extremely good at conditioning the subconscious filters of the people through the educational system, controlled media, and the "public security" system which punishes those who dare to cross the line. The party makes sure that, before anyone crosses the line, he will consciously be aware what he is doing and the accompanying risks. Under such a system, most people consciously practice self-censoring to avoid troubles.

Once, I had an interesting conversation with a friend who was a television producer in China. When I mentioned the government control and manipulation of information, she looked surprised.

"There is no government control. I can put whatever I want on the air," she argued.

"How about letting me debate someone tomorrow night on the evil of one-party dictatorship?"

She was stunned.

"You know where the line is," I argued. "Everyday, you simply censure yourself, which is the saddest form of censorship."

She obviously realized the problem and changed the topic.

Her subconscious filters were so finely-tuned that she did not even realize that she was nothing but a party organ broadcasting propaganda to the population. She, like many other Chinese people, thought that they were free as long as they did not cross the lines, not realizing that was exactly the definition of lacking freedom.

Americans have their own political indoctrination problems, which are known to the pros as the defining game. Since it is impossible for voters to know what a candidate is all about, a certain level of simplification (to be distinguished from abstraction) is needed. Making the desired simplification stuck in the minds of the voters is the name of the game.

When we are awake, the subconscious filters remain on high alert to take out unwanted information, but when we are asleep, the guards come down, causing nightmares when subconscious filters fail to take out unpleasant information. To reach subconsciously suppressed memories, psychologists use techniques such as hypnosis and dream analysis, but the revealed information is still a cleansed version, and often so garbled that even professional psychologists could not assure the validity of their interpretations.

The power of the filter is profound and overwhelming. When I was young, I held the opinion that Hans Christian Andersen overstated the case in his *Emperor's New Cloth*. How could it be possible for so many people to fail to see something so obvious? After hanging out in the real world for a while, I have realized that Andersen's assessment was quite fitting, as the subconscious filters take out substantial and obvious information unapologetically. People with different background literally see the world differently because of their different subconscious filters.

Since the subconscious filters stand between the conscious minds and reality, it is far more difficult to change a bad habit than to learn something anew. When I first learned to ski, I was told to take a weeklong lesson because if I had learned by myself, I would have picked up bad habits, which would be with me for the rest of my life. It was a wonderful advice.

For the same reason, early education is extremely important[5], because children start to develop their subconscious filters as soon as they are born.

When people form opinions with heavy involvement of the subconscious filters, their arguments tend to be general (e.g., full of clichés), slightly off issue, or shifting from one issue to another. When I interviewed people for jobs, I often played the little game of arguing against the candidate by playing devil's advocate, while observing their mental activities, which were reflected in either their language or bodily movements. When a candidate tried to clarify an issue in preparation of argument, he would get one merit point. If he tried to change the subject when running into trouble, there would be one demerit point. Self-conflicting arguments probably would destroy his candidacy. I was always amazed how effective this little technique was in judging the quality of people.

---

5.   See Chapter 5

When the filter goes into spasm, and indiscriminatively filters out massive amount of information related to unpleasantness, we are in denial. It could be so strong that people deny the most obvious facts. Chronic denials create psychological burdens that prohibit free thinking because of the fear of touching psychological landmines.

Denials bring problems from nightmares to drug addiction. Confronted with continuous contrary evidence and refusing to face reality, we simply have to put up more resources to re-enforce the deception. At certain point, we are in clinical denial—the outright refusal to see truth at all cost—when the body uses every method, from projection, reversal, displacement, to rationalization, to counter the incoming contrary information. The subconscious filters work so hard to deny reality that they throw the baby out with the bathwater. In denial, we lose the basic sense of reason.

Obvious cases of clinical denial often take place in association with substance abuse, because body simply could not produce so much opioids. Quitting drugs, to these people, is almost impossible as the subconscious filters ruthlessly block any suggestion of reduction. Without the so-called "hitting the bottom", nothing would get through.

In the jungles, denial, or refusal to change the existing subconscious filters, increases the accuracy of the natural selection process[6]. In today's society, such mechanism of inflexibility is almost always counterproductive.

The interesting phenomenon is that a certain degree of denial actually helps people to be successful, because it blocks doubts, especially self-doubts, and allows people to have the single-minded determination to succeed.

Clinical denial could be found in many dictators, such as Adolph Hitler, Joseph Stalin, and Mao Zedong, who would not think twice before killing people who dared to be in their way. By studying personal traits of these dictators, it is easy to find out that the problem is that they were not qualified in their positions. After their phenomenally focused and energetic effort to get to the top, which is excellence, they did not have a chance to mature. Instead, their lack of confidence forced them to distrust everyone and treat talented people as their potential enemies. They lived in the quagmire of needing talented people and the inability of

6.   When individuals hold different but persistent subconscious filters, which are passed from one generation to the next by either genetics or education, the natural selection process could take out those individuals who hold the wrong subconscious filters and allow those with the right ones to flourish.

trusting them. Those three aforementioned individuals, after obtaining power, spent the rest of their lives in clinical denial.

Although today's managers do not have the power to kill, some of them would not hesitate to use the most savaging method to deal with employees who dare to challenge them. The problem is almost always caused by the managers' lack of confidence, which, in most cases, is caused by the lack of competence. These managers are typically good at presentations and networking, which is how they become managers. The higher they rise in an organization, the less qualified they are and therefore stronger the denial.

As these managers hire the same kind of people, their organizations begin to reflect their characters, but we are getting ahead of ourselves. That subject is covered in Chapter 4.

There are many ways for us to deal with those problems. One of the most commonly adopted is the support groups. When people with same problems get together, they don't have to hide their weaknesses as much, allowing the subconscious filters to relax. Also, the act of routinely getting together may be taken by the bodies as signals that the threat is over, triggering further relaxation. Alcoholic Anonymous is especially effective because it provides a venue for alcoholics who want to quit but are not strong enough to do it alone to get together and talk freely about their problems. This process is further helped by religion, which put them into a confessing mode, allowing their subconscious filters to relax further. The constant reciting of "I am an alcoholic" forces the issue to remain in the conscious realm, so subconscious filters could not hide the information. Since the biggest problem for recovering alcoholics is that they are still under spell of the same conditions that have gotten them into drinking in the first place, the old filter could be reestablished any time and rapidly becoming dominating, driving them into drinking again. AA's slogan is that members should not try to solve the problem once and for all but work on it one day at a time. They should treat every single day as a separate battle against alcoholism, and should not hesitate to seek support by attending AA meetings and praying.

Not all support groups are benign. For kids, there is no "doing-poorly-in-school anonymous". When children fail to do well in schools and do not get support from their families, they form gangs. Different activities of gangs, such as keeping secrets, developing coded languages, and getting into fights together, give their brains the illusion that they are doing something to handle the situation. Consequentially, the bodies take those actions as signals to relax. Since the original trigger, which is the constant reminder that they are doing badly in school, remains active, they become addicted to gangs. Traditionally, boys form gangs to support one another. Recently, Asian gangs have grown the reputation of accepting girls.

A more benign type of support group activities among children is the so-called "best friend" phenomenon. Facing all the psychological problems, kids no longer have just friends, but best friends—primarily for psychological and emotional support rather than as playmates. These are relatively stable relationships among a small number of kids, typically two, so they could share everything—a signal to their body that they are doing something about their problems. A special type of the "best friend" phenomenon is the early formation of the boyfriend-girlfriend relations, because no relation could be closer than two people sharing sexual intimacy.

In mismanaged companies, I have seen subgroups promoting the interests of their own members over those who do not belong—sort of civilized corporate gangs, but the most common activity is for members to get together to complain.

The best way to deal with the problems is, of course, to take counter-intuitive moves by confronting them head-on. That is not easy to do because, in the first place, the subconscious filters are in the way, making it hard to confront problems that we don't consciously know.

According to the Chinese *qigong* theory, straightening up mind and straightening up body are the two sides of one single task. For instance, when the subconscious filters work overtime to block reality, we are more likely to start binge eating, because food comforts us.

Many *qigong* masters feel that the easiest way to take care of the problems is by taking care of physical problems (e.g., over-weight, alcoholism, drug abuse, etc.) first through rigid physical exercise. After the person gets his healthy body back, he may start meditation, which is the first step to take care of psychological problems. Only at that stage, one may confidently confront his problems and rebuild the subconscious filters to serve him positively. The theory is that an enormous amount of energy is needed to accomplish that task, which is why one would not have such energy without the physical training phase and medication phase.

According to Zeng Zi[7], a Chinese philosopher, one should first perfect his own body, second establish a happy family life, third govern a nation, and fourth right the wrongs of the world[8].

---

7.   Zeng Zi (505 BC–435 BC) was a student of Confucius.

Before leading others, good leaders take care of their own subconscious filters by being brutally honest—not giving their subconscious filters the first chance to start the deceptive process. Winston Churchill, Margaret Thatcher, Ronald Reagan, and Deng Xiaoping demonstrated that trait. They might be wrong, but they were honest and not afraid to stick their necks out. When the issue was important enough, unfavorable polling result would not make them change their policies. They were unpopular at times, confused occasionally, and unsuccessful frequently. Churchill lost to Clement Atlee in the 1945 election because he wanted individualism to flourish in Britain against government control. He lost because the voters, in the addiction lingo, had not "hit the bottom" with their addiction to big government. Thatcher was lucky because the victory of the Falkland War—an event unrelated to her economic reform—gave her a second term. Ronald Reagan fought for decades to weaken the government in vain before voters finally sent him to the White House at the age of almost 60. After Mao Zedong used Deng Xiaoping's mistakes to topple him with the Cultural Revolution and exiled him to a remote village in Jiangxi Province, everyday, Deng Xiaoping circled his little hut hundreds of times cursing those in Beijing and challenged, "Let's see who lives longer." After Mao's death, he was able to return to Beijing to launch his phenomenal economic reforms.

Throughout history, leaders are punished for speaking truth. People might wander why Nicolaus Copernicus, Giordano Bruno, Galileo, and Martin Luther went through all those troubles to be punished. Their lives would have been much easier if they had just hanged around and said nothing, but they were the true leaders, refusing to allow their own subconscious filters to be contaminated. Most of the population, educated as well as uneducated, would consider them crazy and would not follow their footsteps. Despite all the negative side effects of civilization, their counter-intuitive conscious thinking brought us further away from jungle into secure and civilized life.

The late Pope John Paul II has been calling for people to "be not afraid" throughout his life. Of course, to those in denial, slogans like "Just Say No" (to drugs) would not help, because the subconscious filters would simply take out the messages, but for people who are actively struggling, such as Poland's Solidarity Movement, John Paul's message arguably provides the pivotal help in their hour of need. When members of the Solidarity made their determined effort to fight against their own powerful communist subconscious filters, such spiritual sup-

---

8.   Chinese: 修身, 齐家, 治国, 平天下

port was vital. John Paul's success and Nancy Reagan's failure illustrate the power of the subconscious filters.

Although bureaucratic managers treat truth-seeking and truth-telling people as pain, a reasonable society should have a mechanism to promote these people over those incompetent ones who focus on presentation and networking skills.

Reading Jefferson's writings in his later years, one sees Nature's reward to those with lifelong honesty—confident, tranquil, and happy. Einstein died a happy man even when his search for the Unified Field Theory was a total failure.

After the communist takeover, many Chinese people were allowed no chance to accomplish anything. To an outsider, they wasted their best years, but I had the good fortune to know some of them. In China, there was a saying that one might learn more in one conversation than ten years of schooling. Talking to these people, who spent their whole lives secretly extending their understandings of the world and keeping healthy subconscious filters, I had that precise experience. If they had been allowed to run the affairs of China, China would have been the most powerful economy in the world and the best friend of the U.S. today. As history had it, their pragmatism forced them to build cocoons around themselves, and forego the possible contribution they could have made to the world at large. With regret, they died happy men.

The problem we suffer as individuals leads to the problem we have with one another, which is the topic of the next chapter.

3

The Interpersonal Aspect

○ ○

A lie gets halfway around the world before the truth has a chance
to get its pants on.

—Sir Winston Leonard Spenser Churchill

In many ways, lying to oneself and lying to others go hand-in-hand, because they
share the same cause—the badly designed psychological and physiological systems, the double-edged subconscious filters, and the corollaries such as the pursuit of self-interest, laziness, the yearning to be respected for nonexistent qualities,
etc.

The difference, or the special trouble in interpersonal deception, is that we
have to make others believe those lies—not an easy task. If self-deception is like
boxing against a dummy, deceiving others is like hitting a person who may hit
back. We no longer have total control.

The Game Theory, a mathematical discipline, studies this situation quite
thoroughly. Since this is not a mathematical book, we shall not get into the
details. For the purpose of this book, we only need to discuss one special case,
known as Prisoner's Dilemma, in which two people (Prisoner A and Prisoner B)
are arrested and face three alternatives: (1) if both confess, each would be sentenced to jail for three years; (2) if neither confesses, each would get two years; (3)
if only one confesses, the confessor gets one year; and the other four years.

Action	A's sentence	B's sentence	Total
Both A and B confess.	3 years	3 years	6 years
A confesses; B does not.	1 year	4 years	5 years
B confesses, A does not.	4 years	1 year	5 years
Neither confesses.	2 years	2 years	4 years

A quick glance of the "Total" column reveals that "neither confesses" is the best choice because the two prisoners (A and B), collectively, spend the least amount of time in jail, but by observing "A's sentence" column, we find that confessing is the best way, because confessing would result in either 1 or 3 years, while not confessing results in 2 or 4 years, thus the dilemma.

In order to make Prisoner A look at the "A's sentence" column, and Prisoner B look at the "B's sentence" column, instead of the "Total" column, police would interrogate the two prisoners separately and tell each that the other has confessed, making the prisoners feel that their options are either four-year imprisonment for not confessing or three-year imprisonment for confessing.

One of the applications of Prisoner's Dilemma is that in personal relations, those who want to improve the relations always carry an unfair burden, exposing themselves to exploitation. For instance, in a two-party situation, when Party A wants to improve the relation and the Party B does not, Party B stands to gain because Party B could exploit Party A's efforts to improve the relation. If Party B keeps up the exploitation, at some point, Party A would stop making the pointless sacrifice, resulting in worse situations for both as neither party wants to do anything to help each other. Of course, a better option is for the parties to come to some kind of arrangement so they could help each other. One special example for this situation is marriage, where the one who does not care about the other stands to gain from the one who does.

The same situation exists in multilateral relations. I coordinate a hiking group in Los Angeles. Those who show up late exploit those on time. When waiting, those who arrive on time often claim that they are going to start to show up late the next time.

Generally speaking, Prisoner's Dilemma exists because the best option for the group is never the best option from personal perspective because the best option from personal perspective is to exploit everyone else. It boils down to the reality that, if one person exploits another, he is going to gain until the other refuses to be taken advantage of, at which point, both sides would be worse off than if they have worked together.

So, according to Prisoner's Dilemma, in business organizations, those who work on problems for the company are always at a competitive disadvantage against those who devote their time cultivating relations to promote themselves against problem solvers. When problem solvers do not pose a threat to bureaucrats, the bureaucrats might leave them alone, but sooner or later, problem solvers have to decide whether to challenge the bureaucrats or become one of them. A challenge would induce immediately and mercilessly squeeze by the bureaucrats. There is a good chance that the problem solvers would lose. The common accusations include that the problem solver is not a team player, does not fit into the team chemistry, or lacks communication skills. The bureaucrats are extremely vicious because they are in the reckless self-preservation mode. In other words, bureaucrats make everyone less effective, thus less threatening.

To those who are less competent, playing the bureaucratic game is a necessity because the task of becoming competent is much harder to accomplish.

After bureaucrats successfully make the organization stale, mild reforms could not touch them. To change the situation, top leaders have to break the backbones of the bureaucrats by launching what is known to economists as shock therapy.[1]

Effective leaders personally make sure that antagonistic laws like Prisoner's Dilemma do not dominate their organizations. Ed Deming has pushed for the system under which everybody serves the interests of the customers directly. In manufacturing for example, the assembly line workers can be linked to customers by recording all of their actions to every piece of product through serial numbers. When a customer has a problem with a product, through the serial number, the worker who has made the mistake could be located easily. Deming's hope is that when people worry about customers, they do not have to concern themselves with the internal bureaucratic maneuvers. Deming's ideas made him the management God in Japan, which in no small part enabled the Japanese companies to make inroad into the U.S. from the 1950s. The most prestigious award for Japanese companies is called the Deming Award[2].

---

1.   See Chapter 7.
2.   It is given by the Deming Prize Committee of the Japanese Union of Scientists and Engineers.

To me, calling his method Total Quality Management is a misnomer, because his philosophy is for the companies to establish a link between individual employees and individual customers. Quality management is merely one aspect of it.

When an organization operates under the Deming rules, it could be a wonderful experience for anyone involved. Life is simpler, as everyone worries about the work rather than bureaucratic maneuvers. People operate on the footing of equality. Everybody has the same chance to demonstrate their creativities through innovations. Although managers have to make certain management decisions, there is no doubt in anyone's mind who is to be promoted and who is on the to-go list.

Once, I managed a software development team. Before letting go a non-productive employee, I consulted the entire team one member at a time. Every single person said that he/she was amazed that it took me so long to take action. Under an open system, productive people have no fear and non-productive people know that their days are numbered.

One of the most studied working relationships in the U.S. is that between the presidents and their aides. Term limit gives every president the urgency to get things done, ironically in the most bureaucratic environment in the nation. So we see the demonstration of strong leadership skills. For instance, under the general direction of Ronald Reagan, the so-called Baker-Meese-Deaver[3] troika was largely responsible for weakening government intrusion into people's lives and unleashing the market power. Later, during Reagan's second term, under the weak leadership of Don Regan, the Reagan presidency itself was threatened during the Iran-*Contra* Scandal.

The Baker-Meese-Deaver troika ran into problems when there were conflicting ideas. Since Reagan wanted the conflict to be resolved before reaching him, conflicts had to be sorted out somewhere. In Reagan's case, it was the press. In other words, the battles of ideas were not waged in the Oval Office but in the press. Baker, a skilled press manipulator himself, was partially responsible for the White House that could not hold any secret.

On the contrary, George W. Bush is an exemplary manager, demonstrating order and efficiency. During his first term, Condoleezza Rice, as Bush's National Security Advisor, took on the job of crystallizing the opinions from different sources, primarily those from Secretary of Defense Donald Rumsfeld and Secre-

---

3.   Jim Baker, Ed Meese, and Mike Deaver

tary of State Colin Powell, so Bush could make his decision on those sharpened opinions. Powell's resignation after Bush's first term was probably caused by the fact that he had been consistently losing his argument to Rumsfeld. When the president is in charge, there is no point for people to make their arguments elsewhere, such as in the press.

Leaders should welcome the collision of ideas among subordinates and participate in debates because that is the best way, if not the only way, to produce the best option. Reagan's lack of engagement caused the battles in the press. Jimmy Carter drowned himself in details, making his presidency ineffective. George W. Bush seems to be handling that aspect correctly.

Presidential politics is always leadership in action, in one way or another. In private life, leadership in action is a rare occurrence. Sadly, most people never have a chance to experience it. They spent their lives playing bureaucratic games because of the fear that standing up would cause them trouble.

People of some professions tell more lies than others. For instance, engineers tend to lie much less than sales professionals, because for engineers, lying does not help them solve their problems; while for sales professionals, lying might get them a sale, which is their *raison d'être*. In today's ever increasingly sophisticated world, many industrial sales people do not know whether the technologies would work for a certain client. Their job is to get the clients sign above the dotted lines and let the technical staff take care of the rest. That division of labor creates some interesting stories. When working for Fujifilm, I managed a line of imaging products that interfaced with other products made by GE, Siemens, etc. Once, a sales rep told a potential customer that we could interface with a particular GE product (without checking with me first). The customer called GE. After some trouble locating the right person, GE told the customer that he wanted to call a person named Pujie at Fujifilm. If this Pujie said that it was okay, then it was okay. That story spread throughout the company like a wild fire. Starting from that point, sales reps began to throw my name around as guarantee of delivery, often without checking with me first. Calling them lying bastards in their faces could not stop that practice. (I must say here that many of these sales reps performed their duties exceptionally well; they have all my respect; it has been a privilege working with them; and I have nothing but fond memories of them today.)

Politicians lie. Jimmy Carter brought a new term to Washington—"rafshooney", after his aide Gerald Rafshoon managed to turn Carter's inexperience and incompetence into an indisputable image of honesty and an outsider. In fact, political spinning, or rafshooney, is so rampant that people think that the politicians are lying by default. When some journalists suggested that George W. Bush might mean and do what he said, others were appalled at the possibility that a politician might have just spoken his mind on national television.

Of all places, people probably lie most in courts, where perjury is supposedly a punishable criminal offense. Once, I told the Los Angeles Superior Court that I could not do the month-long jury duty that it was putting me on. After nothing happened, I called the clerk to ask why they still put me on the jury. The clerk told me that the jury room staff probably did not believe what I wrote on the forms, which warned me that if I had lied, the government could prosecute me for perjury. So, I had to make a trip to downtown Los Angeles and the court had to pay me for explaining everything again in front of a judge. Either the court clerks were the least trustful people I had ever met in my life; or wholesale lying was taking place on jury forms.

If normal people are amateur liars in courts, legal professionals are experts. When I first confronted the amount of lying by police, detectives, and government lawyers in order to accomplish "justice" in the fast food fashion, being stunned is an understatement. Lawyers are professional liars because lying is often the easiest way to carry on their business and they usually get away with it. They have developed it into such an art that those who tell truth have difficulties even to get clients, because lies always sound better than the reality, and clients want the easiest way out. The name of the game is often not about winning cases for clients, but feeding them with lies to get fees. In poor areas, where the population is not well educated, this problem is especially acute. Of course, these clients share half the blame. One attorney friend of mine told me that, after she explained the procedure of obtaining green card through work, which was a 5-year process including H-1B, PERM, I-140, and I-485, most clients wanted an easier way out. She had to compete against attorneys who would recommend asylum to these people without telling them the tough interview that they had to pass to get the benefit. Interestingly, these potential clients typically thought that they were good liars and could handle asylum officers. Their problem was that, after they found out that they had underestimated the asylum officers, they were already in the removal process. Among these unfortunate people was a lawyer graduated from Beijing University, masquerading as a clerk in a Chinese company.

Attorneys do not tell potential clients that the passing rate is very low, because very few applicants could satisfactorily answer the questions of asylum officers. When they are denied and automatically put in removal proceedings, the lawyers would tell them that the only move left is to marry an American citizen, but do not typically mention that marrying after a certain point in the appeal process or marrying someone who is too old to consummate the marriage would, once again, get them a denial from USCIS[4].

Facing these applicants, the asylum officers become so tough and allow so few inconsistencies that people who are truly persecuted by the Chinese government are denied and deported.

The best lawyers could manipulate the jury the way they want. The late Johnny Cochran was fascinating in misleading the jury. On national TV, in the O. J. Simpson trial, Cochran managed to turn a murder trial into a trial against racial discrimination in Los Angeles. Throughout the country, the overwhelming majority of the white people thought that Simpson was guilty, while the overwhelming majority of the black people thought otherwise. Cochran accomplished his job—he successfully convinced the jury that in the trial about racial relations, the police was on the wrong side. Instead of being made a villain, he was hailed as a hero and master lawyer. In the American culture, lawyers are proud to have cajoled the juries into drawing wrong conclusions in favor of their clients.

Bill Clinton, a non-practicing lawyer, was a bit rusty in lying when he was deep in his sexual scandal. He mistakenly thought that there was no way for Monica Lewinski to prove their intimacy so he rolled the dice, went ahead to deny the relationship in public, and got Hillary Clinton—his wife—and Madeleine Albright—his Secretary of State—to help explain his case to the public, not knowing that Lewinski had kept a dress that was stained with his semen. The consequence was devastating. Clinton finally gave Republicans in Congress the chance to take revenge for what Democrats did to Richard Nixon.

Throughout human history, mountains of books have been written about interpersonal relations. Take Shakespeare for example. Relations between Hamlet and his uncle, Othello and Iago, MacBeth and his wife have fascinated the world for centuries. Human relations are driven by our biological-biochemical system, subconscious system, the Game Theory, etc., often in the direction against our best interests. In other words, interpersonal relations, just like personal affairs, would go in the wrong direction if we don't cultivate it purposely otherwise.

---

4.   United States Citizenship and Immigration Services

4

The Organizational Aspect

Madness is the exception in individuals, but the rule in groups.

—*Friedrich Nietzsche*[1]

Like individuals, organizations exhibit psychological characteristics, which are the sum of the mental states of the individual members.

Organizations' psychological characteristics are often determined by the leaders. For example, nations—a special type of organizations—demonstrate psychotic behaviors when the leaders make their people believe in falsehood passionately. Again and again in human history, from the French Revolution, to the Russian October Revolution, to Hitler's Third Reich, to Japanese expansionism, to Mao Zedong's Cultural Revolution, mad masses conducted horrendous fratricide and destruction. Those who dared to speak out against the madness by telling the truth that the emperors had no cloths on were often summarily and physically destroyed.

Leaders profoundly influence nations, sometimes long after their death. Thomas Jefferson and his comrades, strongly suspicious of powerful government, established a nation with weak government, separate power, emphasis on individual rights and freedom, separation of church and state, due process of law, etc. Long after their death, these principles remain as fabrics of the American society, and have protected the U.S. from madness. Joseph McCarthy's anti-communist witch-hunt did go far compared to the nightmares that nations had to experience because these principles limited his activities.

Many people say that, in business organizations, companies owe their success to the frontline people who make sales calls or produce products. According to

---

1.   http://www.geocities.com/RainForest/Vines/7157/quotes.html (6/20/2002)

these people, CEOs do little. It is quite true that CEOs and most of the managers do not make any money for the company directly, but these people, together, are tasked to produce the psyche of the organization. When leaders reward bureaucrats by allowing their self-serving practices, and punish innovators by not defending their interests proactively, they produce a bureaucratic culture, making the organization as unlikely to succeed as a drug junkie.

CEOs, at the top of the management tree, are the only persons who can defeat bureaucratic offensives because, without CEO's unwavering support, bureaucrats would eat innovative people alive. There could be a million reasons why a product fails, but consistent failures are always an indication of top leaders' ineptitude. That is why good corporate executives are so hard to find. Take Enron for example. The employees could be doing an excellent job analyzing risks or selling energy derivatives, but when the top leaders tried to strike gold through dishonest means, those honest employees did nothing but exacerbating Enron's damage to the society because they helped Enron pose a legitimate image to the public.

A do-nothing sales rep knows that he could count his days, but a do-nothing CEO might last in an organization for a long time, especially facing a reticent board and stable market conditions, allowing other organizations to take advantage of new opportunities. For instance, when Wal-Mart started to use information technologies to run its mega store chain, companies like K-Mart and Sears did not make any decisive move even when Wal-Mart was clearly displaying strength in the marketplace. A couple of decades later, when the settlement time came, K-Mart failed a couple of quick reform maneuvers and went under Chapter 11, while Wal-Mart replaced Sears in Dow 30.

The persistent inability for companies to find qualified leaders is the biggest curse on the American companies.

In many cases, after entrepreneurs successfully start up their company with their excellence, they often run their organization aground because of their lack of abilities to manage large scale operations. Since they do not understand management, they often hire the wrong "professional" managers for their organizations. Troubled companies with their board unable to find competent managers worsen their conditions by the same process. For instance, in the software development business, when companies look for people to manage their product, they look for what is known in the industry as "exact fit". Since there are so many technologies out there, it is almost impossible for any candidate to have "that exact set of technological experiences" that the companies are looking for. The result is that companies force candidates to make up their experiences for each of the positions that they apply for. The practice is at such an extent that, in software training schools, teachers openly tell the students that they need to make up experiences as they look for jobs to satisfy companies' desire for "exact fit", and practice the ability to say "yes" on all the "do you have experience with…" questions. After they are hired, according to these schools, they can always learn everything on the job. Since more confident people tend to lie less, the policy of searching for "exact fit" has the effect of hiring better liars who are likely to be less qualified. The ultimate problem with the policy is that people with "exact fit" might not be the innovative people that the company needs. In fact, considering the lying factor, by seeking "exact fit", the company has less chance finding the right person than just randomly pick one from the pile of resumes. Companies go through these useless motions because people, especially those working for human resources departments, have to justify their existence. Once, when confronted with the question that I didn't have the "exact fit", I responded to the interviewer (the Chief Information Officer of a company with only quality assurance experiences) with an analogy that he needed a writer. It was not important whether the writer had experience with Microsoft Word or WordPerfect because such skills could be easily learned. It was extremely important, however, whether this person could write. Needless to say, not having any clue how to find out whether a person could write (i.e., managing programmers), the CIO with no programming experience himself had no alternative other than looking for an "exact fit" and reject any candidate who said "No, I have never used that technology". Since he could not tell his boss that he selected the candidate by randomly pulling a resume out of a pile, he had to resort to this laborious but counterproductive method, I only wonder how he would manage this development manager.

In another case, a CEO-to-be, who yawned his way into the interview room at 9 a.m. on Monday morning, was only interested in one question: how many hours I could put into the company. I did not have the heart to tell him that he needed sleep and then a lot of exercise (as he was seriously overweight). I did not get the job probably because I was not excited in spending 12 hours a day in my office, just for the purpose of staying there.

When hiring information technology developers (i.e., software programmers) myself, "exact fit" was probably the last thing I looked for. In fact, the question "do you have experience with such-and-such technology" is by itself a self-defeating question. For people with thorough experience of a competing technology, it is often more truthful to reply "yes" than "no", while "yes" is a lie. The irrelevance is further enhanced by the fact that different technologies are wrapped, or customized in the particular software development environment for the specific applications, which means that only one or two developers need to understand each technology.

The source of the problem is that it takes one to know one. For entrepreneurs without management acumen or badly managed companies to find qualified managers, they are going to be gambling no matter what process they use, because without knowing how teams are effectively managed, they have no way to tell who is going to be effective. Most of the "methods" that these people use are probably worse than random selection.

For instance, some companies emphasize "proven track record" of successes, ignoring the fact that, for midlevel managers, it is impossible to assess their contributions to success or failure. Even for CEOs, being able to succeed somewhere else is no guarantee that they are going to be effective in a troubled organization. True managers understand risks, could see problems before their manifestation, and have the ability to lead the organization to solve the problems. Also, they could see and catch new opportunities. They are not necessarily experts of demonstrating their mistake-free successes, but often more ready to think and talk about their failures. The bottom line is that for anyone who has done anything, it is certain that they have made plenty of mistakes. Incompetent people out there looking for too-good-to-be-true and mistake-free managers may get just that—liars.

Others rely on certifications, such as PMI certification, which is merely an indication that the person is good enough to pass certain exams. For managers, the most important characteristics are leadership skills and innovative spirit. Those exams are not even designed to test those characteristics. In fact, I don't see there is a way to develop an examination to test that, because they just force people to lie about themselves. Incidentally, PMP training does have its value. In every project that I have been involved, I have always train a person (titled project coordinator) to be in charge of the PMP matters, such as keeping a project plan, following up with people on actionable items, making sure that tasks are completed on budget and on time, etc. In my opinion, it is ridiculous for managers to worry about those things. Asking a project manager to perform those PMP tasks is like asking the President of the United States to make sure that Air Force One is sufficiently fueled before taking off.

A common problem for companies is that the top management of these troubled companies typically does not even bother to participate in the recruitment process of the middle managers, resulting in the interesting phenomenon that qualified managers are excluded because of a "chemical" mismatch with the existing team, which is often another way to say "you are too sharp for us", "you make us feel uneasy", or "we don't think that we can contain you".

The outcome of those processes is quite sad. Once I worked for a dot-com. "Joe" was one of the people who was high on my lay-off list because he was simply not productive, but he was so nice to everyone that I did not have the heart to lay him off. When the venture capitals pulled the rug under us, we were all out looking for jobs. Joe was hired by another dot-com as a manager. According to programmers working for him, he turned into a madman, yelling at people all the time and putting stress on the programmers as well as on himself, as if that would make others productive. The horror finally came to an end when the dot-com collapsed.

When unqualified people find managers through "exact fit", "chemistry fit", PMP, or some other metrics, they propagate their problems downward. I am absolutely amazed that no interviewer has ever created a situation so I could argue a point against the interviewer. It is one of my favorite interview tricks, because being able to stand in front of the boss and make firm and convincing arguments based on reason is one of those precious and rare abilities, besides that it is one of the best ways to test the thinking process of the interviewee. When I make up my mind and am about to make a mistake, having a subordinate to argue against my decisions convincingly is probably the most cost-effective way to correct the mistake. In the "real world", any displaying of disagreement with the interviewer in the interview process is a kiss of death. "Team spirit" to these interviewers means "whatever the fuss, you should not be the one causing it".

The teams produced by those metrics could not escape the fate of "blind leading blind". In most cases, they play the keep-the-tradition game because they have no ability to implement anything new. For those qualified people who are hired into these organizations by accident, they don't stand a chance against the bureaucrats. In fact, most of them have to choose to either play the game or be squeezed out.

Every industry, at the top level, always has several successful leaders, who are more often than not selected by the market instead of any intelligent process. When troubled companies are in need of leadership skills, they have to pay astronomical remunerations to obtain the services of these "proven" managers. Even so, there is no guarantee that these managers would be effective in their screwed-up environment.

Large and stable companies such as GE use a different strategy to recruit. They hire people directly off of best universities and allow them to develop inside their organizations over time. There are shortfalls for that strategy because good students are typically good followers but not necessarily good innovators or leaders. These companies could use that strategy because they always need people to carry out their proven business processes and prefer setting up subconscious filters to converting people. Later on, the companies can find the right people to promote. The front-end heavy paying system (i.e., to pay more than the worth of the graduates at the beginning and pay them less than their worth later on) favors new graduates. Smart people would leave these large companies later on unless they are on the track to be promoted.

Smaller companies could not play the game of lifetime employment on new graduates. They have a faster rhythm and need different skills from time to time. To keep up the internal innovative spirit, they must go out of their way to find innovative people with leadership skills.

Almost without exception, successful growth companies make good use of the potential of their leaders as well as their employees. Many work hard in those organizations during critical periods, and they are rewarded accordingly. Years after the experience, they could always recite the stories of those periods with fond memories, not unlike those who worked in the White House. For once in their lives, they were truly innovative and made a difference. Unfortunately, only a small fraction of the working population has the privilege to experience that excitement, because bureaucracy grows like weeds, suffocating creative spirits.

Arguably the most important characteristic of an organization is whether it makes people think independently, i.e., whether it encourages individualism.

When people are encouraged to think independently in an organization and speak their minds freely, the organization has a much less chance of picking up psychological problems. Take the psychotic behaviors of nations for example. Hitler got to the top of German politics partially because he gave the German people the false sense of confidence and power at the time of inept leadership and disastrous national economy. After Hitler successfully shut up those who dared to criticize him, he started to carry out his madness unhindered. Many of his believers ended up dying for him. With the Cultural Revolution, Mao Zedong gave the Chinese people the false hope of uprooting the bureaucratic practices of Liu Shaoqi and Deng Xiaoping through violent means. Any voice of opposition was mercilessly suppressed. When Liu Shaoqi, Deng Xiaoping, and their apparatchik were successfully pushed aside, Mao Zedong sent his "revolutionary youth" to the countryside to be "reeducated by the peasants", as the Great Helmsman put it, and wasted an entire generation.

Joseph McCarthy was largely a failure compared to Hitler and Mao, because of the U.S. constitution that, among other things, granted free speech to everyone. So sooner or later, someone would speak up and point out that the emperor had no cloth on. By a Senate hearing, McCarthy was pushed to the ash heaps of history.

For those leaders who could not make an organization productive, they focus on cultivating their images to both insiders and outsiders. After all, for them, it is much easier to cultivate images than working on the substantive issues. For instance, the Chinese government has been successfully convincing the majority of its own people that China has a democratic political system, while it has long given up the effort to persuade the international community of the same nonsense. After the Tiananmen Square Massacre in 1989, the Chinese government has been using the economic success to indoctrinate the Chinese people that Western style democracy would ruin the Chinese economic development by introducing instability. Many Chinese people, especially the new rich, strongly believe that argument.

My television producer friend in China was essentially brainwashed by the government to the point that she believed that China had free press. The government, which runs all the media outlets, makes sure that only this kind of people are entrusted to produce TV programs.

The task of implementing self-deception into the minds of the people is often quite easy because people have a tendency to accept the excuses so they don't have to worry about the problems. With the addition of patriotism, it is not hard for the Chinese people to believe the government's propaganda. The same situation exists in many U.S. companies where they have little trouble convincing their employees that they work for the greatest company on earth. Many organizations are more successful in image making than doing real business, especially with the conspiratorial cooperation of Wall Street. For instance, Enron's management did such a good job convincing its employees that Enron was a great company that even after Enron's demise, many Enron employees still insisted that Enron was one of the finest companies on earth, despite the contrary evidences that Enron hid the debt, manufactured revenue through irregular accounting practices, and conducted fraudulent practices to rig the energy price that exacerbated an already severe energy crisis.

In other places, I have seen employees spending their pocket money to buy stocks of their companies while a 10-minute research on Yahoo! Financial could produce some serious questions.

To outsiders, organizations try to project certain images to help their business activities. Since coming to the U.S. , I had believed that ACLU[2] was to defend and preserve the individual rights and liberties against every kind of abuse, especially government abuse. Its most successful arena was the judiciary system, where it had righted many wrongs. That image began to blur when the U.S. government accused a Los Alamos National Lab scientist Wen-Ho Lee of espionage without sufficient evidence. Contacted for assistance, an ACLU official responded, "what if Lee is guilty?"[3] Would ACLU have helped if Lee had been an African American instead of a Chinese, actually a Taiwanese? In every single circumstance involving Chinese that I had known, ACLU had refused to help. Now, I have a new image of ACLU that it fights for individual liberty, but probably not for the individual liberty of the ethnic Chinese people.

Projecting the right images is an important component of product marketing in the business world, because it makes the customers feel that they are buying from a high quality company, becoming a member of a prestigious group, etc., according to the images that companies successfully project. In the political world, the reality is that people would not be elected without professional image-making by using the same techniques such as polling, focus group studies, and market segmentation. In both cases, image making is largely perception-making, if not deception-making. It is aimed at those who need simplified messages. Competent managers do not practice internal image-making in the organization. I have always found that one of the most effective ways to inject confidence is to be honest with the employees about the state of the company, good and bad, but that won't work in politics or bureaucratic companies because admitting problems would give the opponents the chance to attack.

Generally speaking, there are two types of organizations. One is the so-called growth organizations; the other stable organizations, which is known to Wall Street as cyclical organizations because their stock prices go up and down with the Wall Street boom-bust cycles.[4]

---

2.   American Civil Liberties Union
3.   C-SPAN broadcast of a UCLA event on January 20, 2002
4.   Here, we take the Wall Street practice of ignoring other types of businesses, such as stable mom-and-pop businesses and the imploding companies.

Growth organizations make it in the marketplace by finding a niche. Wal-Mart and Microsoft used to be growth companies. Wal-Mart stopped being a growth company when they stopped making one-day or quarterly sales record in the U.S. Microsoft stopped being a growth company when it reached market saturation. Growth companies grow their businesses by doing something better than their larger competitors (e.g., Wal-Mart taking away K-Mart's customers) or starting a brand new business (e.g., Microsoft taking advantage of the new personal computer's operating system market). In either case, on their way up, growth organizations are relatively insensitive to the economic cycles. Their financial numbers, including stock prices, go straight up or hold steady through bear markets. In that sense, one might say that the stock market crash of 2000–2002 proved that Microsoft had become a cyclical company because it lost half of its market value from the end of 1999 to the end of 2002, while Wal-Mart enjoyed its last period of being a growth company by keeping their stock price steady for the same period. Today, both companies are cyclical because their sizes have reached the point that they are enjoying the advantages of existing customer bases, economy of scale, and well-established business practices. Their smaller competitors frequently take advantage of their inabilities to move fast in response to the changing market conditions.

The most significant characteristics of growth organizations are their innovative and leadership quality.

Innovation is the livelihood for all growth organizations, because it is the only weapon for them to survive the onslaught of their established competitors. Leadership's grand innovative visions are empty dreams without the daily innovative activities of the employees. For growth companies, status quo means giving bigger players the opportunity to run them out of business. Even with innovative spirit, it is not easy to eat the lunch of the bigger players who have the advantage of existing customer bases, the economy of scale, etc.

When Microsoft was small, it was lucky to have skipped the initial customer gathering stage, because it benefited from an IBM[5] mistake. In the early days of IBM PC[6], IBM failed to recognize the value of the operating system and outsourced it to Microsoft, an unknown company at that time. With that luck, Microsoft inherited IBM's customers and then the customers of the clone manufacturers such as Compaq (now part of Hewlett Packard) and Dell.

---

5.   International Business Machine
6.   Personal Computers

Once Microsoft became big, it started to use its size to lean on the innovators. It tries to take advantage of people who are not even trying to take its business away. For years, Microsoft has implemented a strategy to expand its business by identifying successful products, e.g., Netscape Navigator, WordPerfect, and Lotus 1-2-3, producing their own version of the software, e.g., Microsoft Internet Explore, Word, and Excel, and then, using its size to sell the product cheaper or giving it away for free. Facing the enormous success of Netscape Navigator, Microsoft started to give away its Internet Explore. In time, and due to several technical mistakes of Netscape, Microsoft Internet Explore took over the market.

It is not easy to take on the abusive industry giant, but not impossible. Recently, Mozilla Foundation is eating away Microsoft Internet Explorer's market share with its Firefox browsers simply because Firefox browsers offer a set of superior functions that Internet Explore browsers do not have. Of course, facing Microsoft, Mozilla must have a pocket that is deep enough to continue giving out its browsers for free and find revenues streams from somewhere other than selling its browsers.

Also, industry giant's weight itself is not sufficient to win. Microsoft created MSN years ago to gain ISP[7] business, it could not capture the fancy of the customers who horded America Online. Finally, as the dialup technologies began to lose their steam to high-speed connections and AOL displayed apparent complacency, MSN finally caught on.

In the search engine business, Microsoft did even more poorly. After working on it for years, it could not take away the market share of Yahoo, the industry leader at the time, while Google did exactly that with its superior innovative culture and leadership. One may contribute Microsoft's failure to the cumbersome nature of the Microsoft operating system (i.e., Windows Servers), but the bottom line is still that Google, which uses its own proprietary system build from ground up, is a more innovative organization than Microsoft.

After years of trying, Microsoft's Media Player could not replace Real Player[8], which is still the standard player of streaming videos.

Leaders have to take on two tasks. First, they have to recognize innovative people and hire them into the team. Second, even with innovative people, leaders have to constantly cultivate the culture of the organization so every member is

---

7. Internet Service Provider gives user the entrance to the Internet. America Online was one of the early ISP successes.
8. It is produced by RealNetworks, Inc.

motivated to innovate. Good leaders understand that keeping up the innovative energy in organizations is like swimming against the tide (i.e., Prisoner's Dilemma, organizational psychological filters, etc.) that idleness means moving backward and allowing the bureaucratic force to overwhelm the innovative spirit. The larger the organization, the harder the top leaders have to work against the bureaucratic tendency because it is harder for them to know what is going on at the bottom level of the organization, and for innovative voices from the bottom to be heard, but easier for bureaucratic force to suppress different voices. Also, large businesses often run on the tradition or proven business practices, making it more difficult for managers to handle the conflict of tradition versus the need to innovate. Often, the pressure to conform overwhelms innovations, especially when managers think that they are going to make the same amount of money regardless whether they innovate, which could put the existing business at risk. Before George Fisher took over Eastman Kodak, the bureaucratic environment was such that literally nothing could be done there, which gave Fujifilm, the company that once employed me, a competitive edge.

In my experience, American workers are quite innovative. As a manager, whenever I run into problems, I have always been able to find someone in the organization, often a low-level employee, holding the answer. All I need to do is to go around finding these people, allow them to implement their own ideas if they are qualified to do the work, and give them all the support that I could give. When people are allowed to implement their own ideas, they always work hard and, with support, usually accomplish their goals. That has won me more than my share of enemies because I offend their pride by promoting others over them, but till today I still could not think of a better way to put the right people in the right positions. It is amazing that so few managers employ that practice.

When growth companies hit a certain scale, like Microsoft and Wal-Mart, they need to take advantage of their size by working on their existing customer bases, supply networks, etc. Agreeing with the latest Wal-Mart practice or not, one has to admit that Wal-Mart, as an industrial giant, has continued Sam Walton's practice of keep trying new ideas, although one might reasonably argue that the new generation of the managers have implemented some problematic policies that Sam Walton would never do. Wal-Mart, after Sam Walton's death, is under the second generation's curse, when new leaders have to measure up to Sam Walton's judgment power from his superior learning, leadership, and innovative skills.

As cyclical organizations grow complacent, they increasingly resemble troops under George McClellan rather than Ulysses S. Grant or William Tecumseh Sherman. They are armies with excellent soldiers and could win battles, but do not win wars. Many U.S. airlines, such as UAL[9], have exactly that problem. Confronted by changing environment, they simply could not figure out an innovative way to handle it, giving innovative companies the chance to take their business away.

Since the introduction of new globalism in the 1980s, large companies have been going bankrupt routinely. For those companies that remain afloat, layoffs have become routine. Knowing the problems, cyclical organizations try different ways to become more competitive. Once, IBM tried to break the static corporate structure by routinely shifting people from one department to another. The program was not successful because it replaced one bureaucratic problem (i.e., bureaucracy that is grown in stable organizations) with another (i.e., the bureaucratic process of shuffling people around).

Other companies try to stay ahead by buying successful growth companies, but with today's speed of change, that is no escape from the task of improving and reinventing their core businesses constantly, which is the secret of the success of Jack Welch at GE and Lou Gerstner at IBM.

In that sense, innovative people are needed everywhere, but the culture does not always agree with reason. Once, I took a psychological evaluation when looking for a job. Many questions were designed to get one piece of information out of me: When truth and corporate culture collided, which way would I go? Without a "merge" option, I consistently answered that I would stick with the truth. The result sheet said that I should avoid big companies, and work for small ones. It did not explain the fact that I had happily worked for Fujifilm for six years. As long as the nation thinks that those who tell truth over corporate culture do not belong in big companies, we as a whole have a problem.

In the foreseeable future, competition is only going to intensify for the U.S. companies. For instance, so far, China has been exporting to the U.S. only low-tech labor-intensive goods that the U.S. wasn't making when China entered the picture. Now, technology companies like Microsoft and Oracle have opened their research and development centers in China. With American training, the next generation of Chinese products will compete against the American products in high-tech fields. If the American people fail to compete (evaluated by produc-

---

9.   UAL is the parent company of United Airlines. UAL employees are the majority owner of the company.

tion cost, which equals to wage divided by productivity), high-paying jobs are going to flee, as companies pursue low cost locations to accomplish their tasks. Part of the American wealth in the past has been brought by the innovative premium.[10] Losing it is an unthinkably painful process for the American people.

One key point to observe, in order to predict the American future, is the creativeness of its companies. For companies to be creative, it must make good use of the creativeness of their employees rather than suppress it as many companies are doing right now. In the high-tech job slums since 2001, many high-tech professionals concluded that high tech was hopeless in the U.S. and moved on to other areas such as real-estate brokerage—an enormous waste of the American creative minds. Many former international students returned to their home country to look for jobs—a reverse brain drain in the scale that the U.S. probably had never seen.

Different politicians talk about different ways to promote American businesses so they could lead the next round of revolution. They certainly put their fingers on the right place but the details of their plans are often much less admirable. For instance, in extreme budget difficulties, California Governor Gray Davis talked about spending taxpayer's money to promote biotech research. When I asked him why not information technology, he sheepishly said that information technology had to come back with its own strength. When pushed further, Davis said that the reason for promoting biotech was for the benefit of the aging California population. If I had interviewed Davis for a job, he would not get it because of his fast dancing from one issue (i.e., promoting California business) to another (i.e., serving aging population). He might not have realized that the best way to serve the aging population of California is to obtain the best and cheapest healthcare product in the world, wherever it is made.

Among all political and corporate talks, I have hardly heard anyone speaking about the need to focus on innovativeness of the companies by hiring innovative people and put competent leaders on top to push for innovative spirit.

Besides internal conflict between bureaucrats and reformers, organizations are also influenced by outside forces. If the organization faces tough competition that threatens its survival, it is easier for the reformers to innovate. On the other hand, if the market force is stale and companies do not face any threat, there is less motivation for the board, shareholders, executives, or employees to innovate.

---

10. When an American company is the first company to produce a much needed products, it could overcharge customers before others follow suit.

Under Newton's law, objects accelerate in the direction of the net forces that are applied on them. The same law could be applied to organizations with inside and outside forces pulling in all directions. When the market force is stronger, organizations have a tendency to find an innovative CEO to lead it to renew itself. When market force is weak, bureaucracy would fair much stronger because people would like to do less instead of more.

5

Education

When dealing with ourselves, we face a relatively clean fight, because we don't have to worry about others. If we are determined to solve a problem with ourselves, we can always take care of it with sheer will. For instance, many people have dealt with their alcoholism by quitting cold-turkey and staying dry for years[1].

In interpersonal situations, especially in the group situation with a strong bureaucratic culture, one person's determination is often not enough to convince others to do the same, even if that person is the CEO. When the ball of change finally starts rolling, many executioners would use it as opportunities to pursue their own agenda, which could turn a perfectly designed reform, after implemented through a bureaucratic system, into something that the original designer could not even recognize.

As we have discussed in Chapter 4, an organization takes on its own psyche. Although it is definitely influenced by its leadership, it often turns out to be something other than what the leadership wishes for. For the educational system, the leadership, such as the president of the United States and the governors of different states, often could not get enough parliamentary support to implement their reform initiatives, since every step of the way the teachers have prevailed in convincing the public that the proposed reform is a bad idea.

The problem could be frustrating to the public as well as the leaders. The majority of the American people, on one hand, know that the educational system has problems. On the other hand, the educational system, so far, has been successfully convincing the public that fundamental reforms are not good for the students.

The frustration runs deeper than just the educational system because education is the key to many other problems, such as the drug problems, teenage preg-

---

1.   Quitting cold-turkey is not the recommended method to stop drinking because of the risks of side effects.

nancy problems, teenage single mother problems, generation after generation of perpetual poverty in many areas of the country, etc.

Before the discussion of the educational system, it is useful to discuss the learning process. The information provided here is neither new nor hard to find in the age of Google[2].

Education starts from the first day when a newborn is brought home. The first skill for newborn to learn is to put himself[3] to sleep from the wide-awake state, unassisted. When children fail to learn this skill, it could mean nightmare for their parents. I have heard stories that some parents have to put their babies in the car and drive around the block so the babies could fall asleep. Even that would not solve the problem because babies always wake up in the middle of night. If a baby does not know how to handle the process of falling to sleep, he is going to ask the grownups for help by crying. The biggest problem for the baby is that he would get too excited (through the physical activity of crying and mental activity of getting the adult to hold him) for too many times throughout the night to fall into deep sleep, which is one of the keys for his health. For instance, growth hormones are generated during deep sleep. If the baby could not sleep deeply, he would lack such growth hormone in his body. Also, habitual lack of good sleep and the persistent task of requesting adult attention by crying harder and harder would prevent the baby from developing a happy and mild temper.

A crash course of new-born education could be completed in a few hours via Google. When Wei, my wife, and I took Leo, our son, home from hospital, we decided to train him that skill right away. As expected, the little helpless thing cried almost all night, but we stuck to our plan to whisper in his ears every 20 minutes or so but not to touch him, except for feeding. After the all-night affair, we wondered whether two weeks would be enough for him to learn the ability to fall asleep by himself.

Miracle happened on Day Two, when Leo fell asleep all by himself. He only cried around 3 a.m. when we had to feed him. Three weeks later, he slept through the night without the three-o'clock feed.

Since then, we ignored the rule that required us to put Leo to bed only when he was wide awake. If he was already half-asleep at bedtime, we did not wake him up just so he could exercise the skill of putting himself back to sleep.

---

2.   http://www.google.com
3.   Here, and throughout the book, "he", "him", or "himself", when used in neutral situations like here, could also mean "she", "her", or "herself", and vice versa.

The next battle is over adult's attention when the baby is awake. Many parents do not realize it when they are conditioned by the baby. The process is actually quite simple. When baby needs attention, he would cry. Often, adults would not respond to baby at first. So baby cries harder. At certain point, the adult gives in and goes over to hold the baby. It might not mean much to the adult, but to the baby who has just started figuring out the world, it means that the way to get the adult's attention is by crying. If the adult does not come, it means that he is not crying hard enough.

The worse part comes when the parents want to "change" this belief of the baby. I have heard stories that when adults finally decided to train the baby, the baby cried so hard that he went into shock.

It is actually not hard to do this right. One only needs to make sure that the baby does not establish the crying-holding relationship. For instance, when the baby cries, one could always go to hold the newborn 15 minutes later, regardless whether the baby is crying at that time. The period of fifteen minutes for a newborn is eternity.

The best advantage of not establishing the crying-holding relationship is that when the baby cries, one can respond immediately because there is probably a valid reason for him to cry. Nine times out of ten, the baby is hungry-thirsty[4] or needs new diaper. That is the wonderful beginning for baby to learn to communicate by reason, instead of emotion.

Step three is more demanding than the first two: babies emulate adults. If the adult stay depressed, agitated, or rude, the baby would become depressed, agitated, or rude. That is why yelling at babies or hitting them is never a good way to educate them. One of the signs of depression is prolonged sleeping and disinterest, which could be shown in the form of lack of response to adult, such as not smiling back. On the contrary, if the adult is happy, caring, interested, and active, the baby would, almost by miracle, be happy, caring, interested, and active.

After understanding this, I began to check the happiness of the adults by look at their babies. Adults know how to hide their problems in public, but babies don't. When I smile at the baby and the baby demonstrates active hostility, I can

---

4.   Since the latest theory is to feed the baby in either case, there is no need to distinguish the two.

confidently conclude that there is a problem with the family because normal babies have the tendency of copying others, and return kindness with kindness.

Step Four is the happiness of figuring things out. For instance, when baby starts to make sounds, parents can make a game so the babies would be interested in reading "A", "B", "C", "D"...and "1", "2", "3", "4",...to them whenever the baby sees any. Just remember, babies do not go to work during the daytime and need rest when they are not working. They are always ready to learn so long as it is fun. The key for adult is to remain patient. It might be a long time before babies recognize the difference between alphabets and numbers before they recognize individual alphabets and numbers. In recognizing alphabet and subsequent reading, one has to realize that the purpose is not for babies to learn anything but to train them the habit of figuring things out. That is the fun of pre-school learning—the outcome is irrelevant. There is no homework, tests, or examinations. Everything is for the fun of pursuing but not the goal. Parents should not ruin this period for the baby by being goal-minded, because the babies won't get another chance of this until they are retired, when they could, once again, focus only on the fun of learning, in their tranquility, as Thomas Jefferson put it. Once they are in regular schools, a large part of the studying is for the teachers and the exams.

At this stage, formal educational theories enter the picture. The definitive work regarding pre-school education was done by Maria Montessori[5]. The core of her teaching method is that, with clearly distinguished good and evil, teachers should assist (but not lead) the students to develop their own skills and find their own destinies. The test is that when students finally get underway in life, they would not realize the influence or, indeed, the existence of teachers in their lives. Montessori's "vision of the future is no longer of people taking exams and proceeding on that certification from the secondary school to the university, but of individuals passing from one stage of independence to a higher, by means of their own activity, through their own effort of will, which constitutes the inner evolution of the individual."[6]

On a more technical plane, the Montessori Method produces curious-analytical-communicative children by putting them in the never-ending process of find-

---

5.   Maria Montessori (1870–1952) was, among many other things, an expert of pre-school education.

6.   Maria Montessori: *From Childhood to Adolescence*, Schocken Books, 1973

ing their own interests, analyzing the situation under their own desire, and communicating the result to others continuously.

In southern California, for instance, Montessori schools, that use the Montessori Method to teach students, are widely available and do an excellent work training curious-analytical-communicative children. The father of two five-year-old twin boys told me that he ended up sending one to the San Marino Montessori School. After a couple of years of Montessori schooling, the Montessori student had far superior communication skills.

The effectiveness of Montessori communication-skill training comes from providing children with on-going opportunities to communicate increasingly complex ideas that the children have developed themselves. In other schools and home environment, children are often at the receiving end of such communication and do not get enough opportunities to express the ideas they developed themselves.

The Montessori Method has many benefits. For instance, under the curiosity-analysis-communication model, Montessori kids have a healthy sense of curiosity, which lead them to think more and thus know more.

For children with Montessori's curious-analytical-communicative spirit, elementary school is a breeze. The American elementary schools, compared to the Chinese elementary schools for instance, teach very little knowledge. Parents of these children could ignore the school work and get the children interested in something so they could develop persistently. For instance, if the children show interests and talent in music, parents could put them through a 10-year music program, so when they graduate from high school, they would have had a 10-year experience of something they like and can enjoy for the rest of their lives. Having fun is the key here. Kids should never spend 10 years, for instance, to perfect their skills of using engineering CASE[7] tools. Those wage-making skills could be learned later. In the meantime, the experience should be on something meaningful. Spending 10 years to perfect skills of playing computer games might not be a wise investment of time.

For these students, reading, logical thinking, math, writing, civil discourse, etc., come naturally like breathing. From the first day of entering elementary school, parents could start to enjoy a relationship with the children on an equal footing. From this point on, one could be certain that parenting is going to be an enjoyable experience.

---

7.   CASE stands for Computer Aided Software Engineering.

The problem is with those children who enter school without the curious-analytical-communicative spirit. Many of those children start to develop the loser mentality early on. Rather than developing analytical and communication skills, they develop skills of making excuses. For instance, they refuse to admit that they have problems with their analytical skills, but insist that teachers lack ability to explain things to them clearly. The path of least resistance would soon lead these children onto the alternative ways of handling schools. As curious-analytical-communicative students learn, they spend their time and energy perfecting their evading skills.

As described before, these problem kids would befriend those with same problems and form support groups, benign or not. As they grow older, they would be more skillful in handling the situations. At a certain age, with experience and ability to resort to violence, changing them becomes difficult.

At this point, even if these children run into a good teacher, their outlook is not good, because the only way for teachers to be successful is to make these students admit their problems and think, which are the last things that they want to do. Teachers know that they don't have much chance to change a student whose hormonal systems and the subconscious filters are fully engaged against such change. Smart teachers would resort to other means to solve the problem, typically by giving the students a way out without learning.

Another disadvantage for these children is that their parents do not understand education, so they typically accept their children's excuses and think that the problem is with the teachers. When their children run into good teachers who engage the children by acquiring them to think, they would complain that teachers fail to explain things to them, cover too much materials too fast, give their children too much stress, and implement changes that are not gradual enough. Since these parents typically get headaches when they open a book themselves, their children could not get help from them when needed. On the contrary, good students always have ready resources when they need help. Most of them get such support from their parents.

Some parents, with economic ability and facing problematic children, send their children to boarding schools. Boarding schools succeed by providing the students with totally a new environment that encourages, in fact compels, thinking, by forced homework, forced examinations, or semi-institutionalized upperclassman influence. Once these schools successfully de-educate the students of their old subconscious filters by overwhelming them with the new ones, they could make the students think. Gradually, after years of conditioning, these schools could reform a problematic child into curious-analytical-communicative youngsters or, at minimum, pound enough knowledge into them so they can move on to good colleges. Of course, nothing forced is as good as self-motivated.

Since changing a student requires dedicated personal attention and the right environment, not all private schools are effective in this undertaking. Many private schools, such as religious day schools, are not cut out to do such tough work. Parents should not think that sending their children to a private school is the automatic answer for all their children's problems. Day schools are poor in changing students partly because students still live in the same environments that have created their problems in the first place.

Theoretically, educating parents is another way to end the perpetual cycles of bad education. The problem is that these parents have been bad students in the first place and that each family has its own set of the problems, requiring different solutions. Typically, it requires much more work to convert the parents than the children. That may be why there is so little effort for the educational system to educate parents.

For most problematic students, without money to go to private schools and with parents who do not understand education, public schooling is their only choice. Although all parents conceptually desire their children to be successful, in reality, most of them would do their children's bidding against any teacher who dares to compel their children to think. It is a common experience of teachers that parents of good students normally talk about the problems of their children, but the parents of the bad students always insist that they and their children are flawless. As students perfect their skills of manipulating parents against teachers, it is almost impossible for either side to initiate the needed change.

The current state of the educational system is that teachers, especially elementary school teachers, know the problems of each student, and try to communicate with the parents. The problem is that the parents would not take the necessary initiatives, which often include changing their own behaviors, to bring necessary changes to their children. Without parents' cooperation, smart teachers would not even try.

If changes do not take place, children would master the necessary skills to handle the situations by the process of trial and error. Students build their subconscious filters based on the line that the teachers draw in the sand. Typically, the line is drawn where talking in classroom is tolerated but violence is not. It is quite sad to think that the children get up so early to spend the whole day in schools playing the game of evading learning. As long as these students do not cause too much trouble for the teachers, the teachers would let them pass classes, so these students are shuffled through the educational system. Since talking in classroom is tolerated, in K-12, especially in middle schools, a couple of talking students could drag the whole class down.

To me, it is a good thing that children have a lot of energy. It is a problem, or an indictment of the educational system, when the system could not make the students use that energy to learn. Once, a parent asked me whether he should medicate his son so he would not disturb the classes. I told him that the behavior of his son was much more civilized than that of Ansel Adams, who, after finding piano, went through the rigor of teaching himself piano and music. Facing a hyperactive child, he simply needed to find a good channel for the child to release such energy. Many K-12 teachers spend a lot of time resolving "disciplinary" issues with their students. That is outright ridiculous. But the public school curricula, at least of middle schools and high schools, tie the hands of the teachers, as they could not use, for instance, Montessori Method to teach their students.

High schools take care of the smart followers (straight "A" students). Innovative students would also do fine because high schools do not demand that much. Even if their hearts are not with school work, their learning habit would keep them afloat academically. Some of them may even be straight "A" students.

For those who have been shuffled through the elementary and middle schools without thinking, converting them in high schools could be a daunting task, if not impossible, because in high schools (ninth through twelfth grade), their systems could fight against any converting attempts much more effectively than in elementary schools (first to fifth grade).

First, they know the system by then and are probably experts of the game. Even without the consideration of the knowledge deficit that they have accumulated so far, when teachers require them to think, they are going to refuse instinctively. Now, they have more weapons in their arsenal, such as more skillful ways to disrupt classrooms, and complaining to the authority. If they could not find out a good way to do it, sexual harassment accusation is always an excellent fallback[8], besides other ways to get the teacher handcuffed away by the police. Facing those unpleasant situations, the teachers adopt the realistic policy of "why bother with them", or "let them rot", which seems to be the sensible thing to do and the prevailing method of dealing with troubled students. The high school lines are drawn at a much higher abstraction level and clearly: "If you don't screw

---

8.   Here, I am certainly not claiming that all sexual harassment accusations are designed as revenge against dutiful teachers.

me (i.e., the teacher) personally, I am going to let you be." New teachers, during the orientations, are repeatedly warned, because the school districts do not want to see these cases either. Every male teacher understands his vulnerability every time when he walks down the isle checking the work of a female student with low-cut blouse—he runs the risk of being accused of peeking, which is considered sexual harassment.

Second, by this time, the non-thinking students have figured out something else to do to fill their time. The substitutions range from computer games to sexual relationships to gangs. Their own rating systems (e.g., popularity, parents' wealth, gadgets that they own, girls who give them blow jobs, boys who hang around them, gang associations, etc., but never the grade point average) are also working at this time.

For instance, a friend of mine told me a story after he moved to Arcadia, California. His wife drove a Toyota Camry to pick up their daughter. After a couple of days, their daughter refused to be picked up, because other kids belittled her for the Camry. The interesting point was that his daughter was old enough to know that they could easily afford Mercedes or BMW, but opted out because they didn't want to spend money that way. Still, she succumbed to the peer pressure at school.

Children, especially less confident ones, could not resist the powerful rating system. In poor areas, no teaching of the teachers is as powerful as the self-confidence of drug dealing youths coming to school in sports cars, wearing gold chains, and showing off stacks of twenty dollar bills. There is no way that the tender minds of teenagers could handle the onslaught of popularity contest, sexual relations, gang relations, and so on. Their systems are completely stressed out with the subconscious filters working over time. Drugs, which are more readily available than cigarette and alcohol due to the national drug policy, and drug culture are so appealing that one could only wonder how these non-thinking kids could refuse.

At this point, it is almost a joke to ask high school teachers to pierce through the veil of subconscious filters and change the habit of the high school students. Under the current system, since most of the teachers are playing games, those teachers who dare to stand up would be considered a risk by other teachers. Also, even if they change an unwilling student, the students' families and the environment are likely to change them right back. After meeting one of the model teachers who spent most of his waking hours in school at Arcadia High, I had little doubt why there were so few of them and they were so carefully pick salvageable parents before working on the students.

The dominant belief is that the high school students are no longer educable. If one argues the point, seasoned teachers would counter, "When was the last time you saw a kid coming in at the bottom and leaving at top? Minor adjustments may be possible but not fundamental ones."[9]

College is another critical point. Many remember college as the last time that they are truly free and happy. The curious-analytical-communicative type would do fine in colleges. They might be "C" students, however they have started their life-long thinking. Some of them just try to have a good time in college, but poor grades are not going of stop them excelling in the real world. Others, some 5% of the college student population, use the time to explore the intellectual world. Also, they may not have good grades. In fact, professors understand this phenomenon well, and call it the revenge of "C" students.

For those students who enter top colleges such as Harvard or Princeton, they would have the fortune of hanging out with other smart students, making it more likely for them to explore the intellectual world. If they are in the second-tier schools such as UC Berkeley or University of Virginia, they need to have a stronger drive to accomplish that.

The trouble is that problematic students do not enter those schools. If at all, they go to community colleges, which are simply another world. In community colleges, they are surrounded by students who are not thinking and professors who do not think that they are educable.

It is certainly true that some students would use this opportunity away from home to strike free of their chains and try to make something of themselves. Some of them even manage to enter top tier universities such as Caltech after spending two years in the community colleges, but they are the exceptions.

First, their professors know how these students would react under a request to think. The chairman of the physics department of a community college told me that professors should not require the students to think. Professors should explain everything to the students. He gave me an example of a professor who, in physics labs, would lead the students step by step by telling them which connector to connect and which button to push, which led me to the obvious question, "so the students don't have to think about physics to go through the process." The chair-

---

9.   Many immigrant students who enter from the bottom do exit from top, but the reason for them to enter at bottom is entirely language related. They are top students in all other respects on their way in.

man laughed and said, "This is not Caltech. These people would never understand physics."

Second, these students are less tolerant to the professors than their university counterparts. When a professor actually requires them to think, they would immediately complain to the authority. The most common claims are that the professor could not explain things clearly; the professor does not understand the material; and the professor is outright abusive. The result is that students, when taking physics classes, are not taught to break down real-world problems and conceptualize them in mathematical form before studying it. Instead, students are shown how to solve problem sets in classes, repeat the drill through homework, and pass exams by doing the same thing. For an intelligent person to teach non-physics students physics, he would show them the "mathematical abstraction"-"studying"-"understanding"-"application" process, which is the single most important reason human beings are what we are today, but the community colleges would rather play the game instead, which wastes everybody's time and taxpayers' money. In social subjects, the professors, who are mostly leftist, would indoctrinate students because the students have no chance to put any ideas into practice.

Community colleges are good at one thing—training basic skills. For instance, unlike taking physics or sociology, if a student takes a class of medical equipment operation or automobile repair, he would certainly learn something.

The result is that teaching professors—those who try to make the students think—could not last long in today's community colleges. Career community college professors simply go through same motions, to cover things that are related to but not the essence of the subject. Students are shuffled though just like in public high schools. Since many high school teachers work their way up to teach community colleges, it is a natural outcome.

University professors, who live or die on their research projects or, to be more precisely, on their ability to attract research funding, never present themselves as teachers. University education is conducted by graduate students who also conduct research for professors.

Now, with the understanding of the educational process and the educational system, we can discuss the problems that are related to children's education.

For most problematic children, the first problem, which is also the first key to solve the problems, is parents' failure to recognize the importance of early education. Today, with the thorough penetration of Google, awareness should not have been a problem, but oddly enough, most parents, including many well-educated and successful people, do not understand how to conduct early education. People from all walks of life, from professors to lawyers to company executives, have told me that children are what they are (interpretation: early education is useless). Some told me that the way to deal with baby crying all night is to hold him and the baby would stop crying in a year or two. Closer observation always reveals that these parents are conditioned by their children. For instance, some parents yell at their nurses when their children cry, forcing the nurses to hold the children whenever they cry. In the end, their children are spoiled and unhappy.

They have never seen the efficiency of an expert who can change the nature of a child right in front of people's eyes. Under correct guidance, I have seen a fifth grader moving from being one of the worst students in the class to one of the best within one year. Maria Montessori has demonstrated how easy it is for schools to change students in wholesale fashion.

Without proper pre-school education, in poor areas as well as rich, children enter elementary school at a distinctive competitive disadvantage. Since the elementary schools do not respond well to the "I will be nasty until you yield" mode of communication, the children would quickly find that their normal mode of maneuvering does not work any more. Without the curious-analytical-communicative spirit, catching up is simply an impossibility, because those with the spirit would move faster and at a higher acceleration.

The educational system exhibits unique characteristics. Among the systems that are described in this book, it is not only the most isolated and self-enclosed system but also the most deceptive. One may argue that the two are connected. That is the second key for solving the problems.

If education were a business, where people would pay money for service, schools would be competing for students by providing better education with better teachers and better teaching theories. In these schools, true educators who change the students for the better through sometimes painful but constructive processes would be paid higher salaries and those who fail to convert students would be dismissed.

As one of the last relics of the Keynesian big-government scheme that the free market revolution failed to penetrate, the educational system has so far managed to escape reason. In the business lingo of Ed Deming, the problem of the educational system is the isolation of producers and customers. In economics lingo, the third party payer system made teachers' performance irrelevant to their reward.

Certainly, in a free society, people are free to put their children in private schools, but those parents would have to pay twice for the schooling of their children, once through paying taxes and again by paying tuitions and fees. For many parents, private schools are beyond their affordability, making public schools their only option. Therefore, public schools have a *de facto* monopoly on education.

In a monopoly, things happen according to the best interests of the bureaucrats rather than students. For instance, teachers are paid according to a strict pay scale, depending only on the teachers' years of service and education level. Performance is not a factor.

After teaching for one year, K-12 teachers get their job security. It is then practically impossible for schools to get rid of them for poor performances.

Teachers, like the rest of us, live in the free society. Private companies are free to use higher wages to entice better teachers to leave public schools.

The result is that the good teachers are likely to leave, but the bad teachers, with their *de facto* job security, would remain, partly because they could not find better jobs.

When teachers' job and income do not depend on performance, they focus on their own interests and do the least to the customers (i.e., students and parents). Statistically, teachers whose SAT scores are above the 50th percentile have a very small chance of being K-12 teachers for long.

Tenured teachers know that their jobs would be at risk or at least they would have to work much harder if the educational system is exposed to market forces, because after years of noncreative repetitive work, they have lost their ability to adapt to new things. The result is that the teachers associations, which are financially supported by their members, are ultra-sensitive and ultra-reactionary to the slightest reform suggestions. Teachers associations have made arrangement with schools that a teacher could not opt out of paying association fees.

When teachers don't like certain politicians, such as California Governor Arnold Schwarzenegger, they can put on year-round ad campaigns against them. No other organization in the country has that kind of financial power. In the end, teachers normally get their way. Most politicians would give in to the teachers' demand and reframe from reforming the school systems.

Teachers do give politicians a way out. If politicians work out an increase in educational funding, politicians and teachers would all come out to claim victory in the name of students, as if funding increase indicates the system improvement. That is why we have so many education presidents and governors, while the problems are passed from one generation to the next.

Once, I was with a group of teachers and a state representative, talking about the problems of the educational system. They all complained about the problems and said that the government should spend more money. I ventured a comment that the government monopoly of education might be the problem, and asked whether they thought that the introduction of market mechanism would help. These teachers immediately switched to another mode and claimed that the educational system was the greatest thing under the sun that it should not be tinkered with.

Teachers often make self-contradictory arguments. On one hand, they think that it is impossible to "change" students. On the other hand, they would agree that even troubled kids are not "bad". If you ask a California "special ed"[10] teacher about her students, she would tell you that they are all good kids. Those just out of juvenile detention centers normally have no problem recognizing what is right and what is wrong. When given an opportunity, they do the right things. The problem is the classroom atmosphere, which makes kids think that learning is un-cool; disruption is brave; and not paying attention to teachers is a demonstration of courage. It is absolutely fascinating to see some of the worst "special ed" kids, who are often the smartest, failing to be cool because they are genuinely interested in the subject, and could not help themselves when they yell at those who disrupt the classroom. Alas, that does not happen often. The norm is that when teacher turns her head, the next thing she smells is pot.

The author personally likes the malcontent spirit of these students. The trouble is that their families, their environment, and especially their schools could not guide them to use their malcontent in the right way, so they use their creativity and malcontent to develop ways to handle the system.

These kids are psychologically twisted by the system. When confronted by pressure from authority, their brains are immediately switched to the "not talking" option in Prisoner's Dilemma, but when teachers, in a friendly manner, slip them the cheapest toys, such as a couple of baseball cards, they would pretty much tell anything.

People with reasonable experience with these kids may agree with me that these kids yearn for care and guidance, but their families, friends, schools and the justice system convert many of them from amateurs to professional criminals.

---

10. In California, "special education" is a government educational program for persons with disabilities. In reality, "special education" (or "special ed") programs are filled with children from juvenile detention centers and teenage mothers.

In the meantime, teachers are universally negative to alternative educational theories. That is the third key for solving the problems.

The Montessori Method is a problem for teachers because it points out the problems of the current educational system and provides a simple solution. Proponents of the Montessori Method could simply challenge opponents to visit the schools and compare, but educational "experts" try to discredit the Montessori Method, which is why reading papers on education could be a frustrating experience. In her native country of Italy, Montessori was treated as the enemy of the educational system. After she was forced to move to the U.S. , her efforts have never received support from the official educational system and largely remain an underground movement. The educational "experts" never stopped discrediting her. After her death, Rita Kramer wrote that Maria Montessori was "no longer considered a major influence in education, but a historical relic," when she died.[11]

Montessori insisted on clear identification of good and evil. If the educational system is put to that test, one might reasonably argue that the system is evil, because it takes the taxpayers' money to serve the system itself rather than the students.

Modern schools often argue that everything is valid. As multiculturalism goes, all cultures are equally valid, so Chinese *feng-shui,* for instance, is equally valid as Einstein's theories of relativity. Anyone who dares to say anything against such teaching is a racist, fascist, rightist, sexist, and do not deserve to live in this world.

That goes against the Montessori curious-analytical-communicative spirit, because the result of any analysis is opinions. Communication of different opinions leads to open comparison of things, which is civil discourse. For instance, compared to Einstein's relativity, one may opine that *feng-shui* is fundamentally nonsense.

The Montessori Method is powerful because it makes sure that students individually work on things that lead them to their next level of understanding. Conventional schools feed the same materials to all students. For some, the materials are too difficult; for others, too easy; and for most, inappropriate. That is the typical outcome of a system that is designed for the benefit of the teachers instead of the students.

If the Montessori Method has truly become a relic, the Montessori schools should not have flourished. The reality is that the public school teachers have prevailed in convincing many that the Montessori Method is a relic. Those who dis-

---

11.   Rita Kramer: *Maria Montessori,* G.P. Putman's Sons (1976)

agree know that they could not win the public debate, so instead of trying to change the public educational system, they fund Montessori schools by sending their children there.

One of the most powerful weapons of the teachers associations is their use of Marxist class struggle theory. Their propaganda has caused serious frustration and resentment in the society. Seeing that rich people could send their children to private schools, go on to private universities, and get better jobs, poor people who typically do not understand the problems are resentful of the rich instead of the public educational system.

Teachers associations, with their best public relation experts that money can buy, understand this resentment and make the best use of it. When voucher measure was voted in California, it was soundly defeated, because teachers made a successful argument that such measure was the conspiracy of the rich for the rich, who, already sending their children to private schools, wanted to use taxpayers' money to educate their children. In other words, vouchers would become public subsidy to the rich.

The voucher supporters, in the midst of the resentment, could not prevail with their argument that rich people, who are less likely to take their children out of public schools and send them to private schools, are less likely to use their vouchers. However, the frustrated parents who live in poor areas with bad schools are most likely to take advantage of the measure and send their children elsewhere.

In a free market, vouchers would create the best opportunities for entrepreneurs to establish private schools in poor areas because it is the easiest way for them to make money. When the exodus from these bad public schools start, the schools would be forced to give up ridiculous policies such as teachers' fixed pay scale to attract better teachers and get rid of those sub-par teachers regardless how long they have been with the system. Failing to do that, public schools would lose so many students to the point of being bought out by the private schools. Teachers associations would not let that happen, so when the voucher proposition was put to vote, they used the public frustration and Marxist class struggle theory to have the poor and the lower middle class to defeat arguably the only thing going for them.

The reformers resorted to the next best thing and called it "no child left behind", which is no equalizer at all. The measure intended to improve the educational system by making schools accountable through standard examinations of the students. The measures against inadequate schools are questionable at best.

The law carries some negative measures as well. In the name of keeping the quality of the teachers, it made it harder for anyone in mid-career to enter teaching profession, even if they accept the bottom pay rate.

In addition to Montessori and voucher, new technologies have opened new doors for educational reforms, which is the fourth key for solving the problems. One of the options is to reform the educational system by separating the information transfer and education. Students can get information through computerized information systems, while the teachers are around to solve personal learning problems, and focus on, for instance, the individual problems to understand the power of Shakespeare rather than the understanding of his words. With 70 million students in schools[12], a few dollars per student per year could build quite a decent system that everyone could access through the Internet. The availability of ideas is a powerful thing. Otherwise, the Chinese government would not have spent so much money putting China behind a firewall blocking, among other websites, MIT.edu[13].

Powerful teachers associations have produced a weirdly stable educational system. In Los Angeles County, for instance, five minutes away[14] from a high school that routinely sends some 50 kids to UC Berkeley every year, the dream of the student body of another high school is to join their parents in business such as mowing lawns and working on constructions sites, so they could party during the weekend. To them, colleges and higher paying jobs are unreachable. The wise thing to do is to be realistic—being happy with what they have. These people, believing in the teachers associations and resenting the rich living next door, overwhelmingly voted against the voucher measure and therefore upheld the *de facto* caste system.

Since the vested interests are determined to resist the slightest reforms, we have to wait for a "shock therapy". Some describe shock therapy as facing a tiger with one bullet. You either kill the tiger with that one bullet, or become his lunch. So far, no president of the United States has dared to take that shot against the powerful teachers unions on behalf of the students and parents.

---

12. *U.S.A Today,* 5/9/2000
13. The website of the Massachusetts Institute of Technology is making all MIT classes accessible by public via the Internet, free of charge.
14. According to Yahoo Map

We are waiting for a single-minded and suborn politician like Thatcher or Reagan to reform the educational system. When George W. Bush entered the White House, he wanted to push for the voucher system. Seeing the tiger, he backed down.

Besides the public, the educational system is tasked to educate the next generation of creative elite.

The first level of educated elite, who are to become the leaders of the society, is composed of university graduates. In order to make families and students happy, and cover up deficiencies (e.g., lack of professors' interests and attention in education), universities have watered down their curricular and the grading system. Careerist professors are happy to do that because it makes no difference for them to give an "A" or "F". Only those who care about education have a hard time giving out inflated grade for watered down curricula.

Today's value of college degrees is questionable. For instance, a friend of mine got her business administration degree from University of Southern California without taking *any* mathematics class.

As another example, a cousin of mine, who was an international student from Hong Kong, went to Cal Poly Pomona. Before graduation, the school required the students to pass an English composition test. His English composition skills could be described, at best, as a disgrace, but miraculously, he passed, so did his fellow international students whose command of English was even worse. The school used the examination to address the public resentment about the poor writing skills of the graduates, but by allowing substandard students to pass, the test was merely a bureaucratic charade, designed to deal with problems through bureaucratic means rather than solving them by actually improving these students' English.

A special group of undergraduate students had my attention at the University of Virginia, the pre-med, pre-law, and pre-biz students. From pure academic perspective, they were the most ignorant students on ground[15], as they cared nothing but grade, and refused to do anything that might not contribute to their grade. Interestingly, as I found out, they were not stupid people. At the University of Virginia, I called them the ignorant. Now, still regretting their failure to explore the intellectual world, I call them realists. They focused on the grade because they needed that to get into med, law, and biz schools; they did not

---

15. Mr. Jefferson preferred to use the word "ground" to "campus" for his University.

spend time on anything else because they didn't see a reason why they should sacrifice partying and having a good time. To them, exploration might put their careers at risk, so pragmatic people would not attempt that. I once joked that they were making sure that they didn't fall in love with anyone (e.g., literature or physics) so they could marry the daughters of their parent's business associates (i.e., med, law, and biz schools).

At least, when compared to me, they knew what they were doing and had a realistic assessment of the university. On the contrary, I naively thought that the school would be fair with me.

There are two types of graduate students, the paying and the paid. Paying students include those in medical, law, and business schools and those in many master degree programs. Paid students include all those who conduct teaching and research.

Schools treat paying student no differently from the undergraduate students—as a necessary evil, but treat paid students strictly as cheap labors. Many American students would not subject themselves to the maltreatment and would not get into faculty track graduate studies.

In order to keep the universities financially afloat, they recruit foreign students to fill their budget gaps. The extent is quite phenomenal. Once, I visited a physics department in Brooklyn, NY. Chinese was used in department happy hours because most of the students as well as professors were more comfortable speaking Chinese than English.

The weapon of professors against the graduate students is the so-called "academic freedom" under which they can use a student for five years and refuse to give him even a master's degree.

The tenured professors have absolute power in the universities, as they vote on all important matters. Absolute power brings absolute corruption, which is what happens in the universities. For instance, since tenured faculties vote on who to grant tenure, there is no way that they are going to allow a reformer who might damage their vested interests to join their ranks. Today's universities are governed by oligarchic systems that have been used by communist countries, known as "rule by politburo". Since these university politburos have one shot to grant tenure to professors, they are extremely careful.

If a person at mid-career decides that he wants to teach K-12, he may do that if he has no problem with bottom pay, but he would have virtually no chance to become a university professor.

Interestingly, most of the professors, after decades of being underpaid as graduate students, post doctoral fellows, and assistant professors, become ruthless exploiters of others after they get tenure.

The result of such graduate education, including failure to attract qualified American students and failure to allow graduate students to explore, is that the present PhD population is not statistically any wiser or more profound than the general population.[16]

Largely due to the behaviors of the universities, American students shun graduate studies of arts and sciences today, because realists won't voluntarily be abused. Only the true lovers, in a religious sense, enter those fields of study. As the American society, including universities, government research institutes, and private companies, gets its research staff from graduate schools, especially the PhD population, we see an internationalization of those positions.

Many, especially the academicians, claim that the American students are not good at or dislike arts and sciences. They have the high school grades as proof. But my observation is different. If universities could reason with people and treat the graduate students as elite rather than cheap labor by paying them decent salaries and allowing them to explore, I am sure that there will be enough American students willing to spend a few years to teach, explore, and research.

The solution of the college problem is different from K-12.

Thomas Jefferson has suggested a solution for undergraduate education. He wanted the University of Virginia to have an open-door policy, allowing students to decide when to attend and when to leave.

The solution for the graduate level education is more complex. First, universities should break the caste system. Outside military, universities are the only place where people are ranked—as undergraduate students, graduate students, post-docs, assistant professors, associate professors, and full professors. Outside military, nobody is addressed by their titles. In the business world, which is run by dictatorship and demands absolute efficiency, people address each other by their first names.

The university education, according to Allan Bloom, should be something that "friendly men, educated, lively, on a footing of equality, civilized but natu-

---

16.   In other words, if you pick 100 PhDs and 100 people from general population, you will find the same number of profound people from either group.

ral, came together and told wonderful stories about the meaning of their long-ing."[17]

The problem of inequality could be solved by abandoning tenured professorship. As undergraduate students go to classes for education rather than grade or a sheet of paper (i.e., diploma), educating professors should be allowed to teach. Universities could lease spaces to those who attract research grant. These researchers could hire assistants in open market, including, but not exclusively among, the student body. No title of any kind is necessary under this system.

First, teachers would be able to stay in today's universities. Second, researchers could do their research without masquerading as professors. Third, without issuing any grades and diplomas, professors don't have to water down their curricula or inflate their grades, so today's realists may have a chance to actually get an education. Fourth, without the suppressive system from graduate level up, more Americans might want to stay in universities to teach or research. So, fifth, we might finally obtain equal footing in universities, which is a necessary element in producing the next generation of creative elite.

Just like in K-12, all existing professors, who represent the vested interests, would do everything they can to fight against the reform. Anyone who doubts their power should pay attention to their ability of convincing the State Department to issue visas to foreign students to keep the flow of the foreign cheap labors and keep universities financially afloat. In 2005, it is easier for foreign students to get American student visas than before 9/11.

Like K-12, the only treatment that has the realistic chance of succeeding is the "shock therapy" . Since the public is less ready to do anything drastic to the universities than to K-12, it is not likely to happen.

If we apply Newton's law that objects accelerate in the direction of total force, teachers are much stronger than parents and students, resulting in a system that serves the interests of teachers instead of students.

The change could come by, again from Newton's perspective, making parents and students stronger, so the system could tilt toward students. As long as teachers put up effective campaigns against any kind of reform, such as voucher, and as long as parents do not become stronger pulling toward their side, the educational system will not change.

---

17.   Allan Bloom: *Closing of American Mind,* p.381, Simon & Schuster, 1987

Public education should have been an equalizer, promising the children of the poor theoretically the same opportunities as the children of the rich. Decades after its implementation, statistically speaking, the poor are still poorly educated, while the rich are better educated. The success of the class struggle theories employed by the teachers is an illustration of such resentment and frustration by the poor and the lower middle class. Year after year, poor kids drop out, and enter the workforce at the rock bottom by doing things that the rich kids would never care to do.

The joke is that the teachers, as well as Keynesians, claim that they are on the side of the poor against the rich. It is not hard to convince the poor because they are normally bossed by better-educated free market believers. It is easy to make the poor resent whatever their bosses believe.

Free marketers lose their argument because they do not pretend to be on the side of the poor against the rich. In fact, they often seem to argue for the rich by pointing out that they are the winners in the free market system. The poor do not like to hear that.

When teachers tell the poor that voucher is just another scheme by the rich against them, they believe it.

The sad fact is that the inadequate educational system makes it possible in the first place for the teachers to take advantage of the rage of the poor against the rich. Without proper education, they could not make an independent judgment, and may be teachers' foot soldiers generation after generation.

6

Business

Among the systems that are described in this book, the educational system favors service providers the most (vis-à-vis service receivers); the business system favors service receivers the most (vis-à-vis service providers). By looking at the business system, we might gain some confidence in the possibilities of reforming the educational system. One of the problems of today's world is that people are so specialized that they only see a narrow field throughout their careers, often prohibiting them to see the hope right around the corner.

In the business world, it is common place for small companies to squeeze industry giants into bankruptcy. Any complacent company gives its competitors clear chances to take advantages of it. Take McDonald's Corporation for example. Once, in 2002, I went hiking with a friend, ended up at a McDonald's, and ordered two cheeseburgers as snacks. It was the first time in some three years since I had stepped inside a McDonald's. The burger was so dry and bun was so old that the experience shocked me. Then, when I heard the news that McDonald's was forced to close 175 stores in November 2002, after its stock price dropped from almost $50 to $17, I was not surprised.

The fact that marquee names in the U.S. are frequently merged, acquired, or driven into bankruptcy is the clear indication that the market mechanism is working. In other words, if we see that schools routinely fail because parents exercise the power to send their children elsewhere, we will subsequently see that our children are properly educated.

From professional studies to the popularities of Dilbert, reasonable people may conclude that American companies are run by inadequate managers, but, at least to me, that limitation is caused by the quality of people, not the system, which, under the protections such as anti-monopoly laws that forbid unfair competition and SEC rules that governs securities and exchanges, works in most respects. If anti-monopoly laws are applicable to the educational system, breaking up the school system would be the easiest case for the Department of Justice to prove in court.

The popularity of MBAs and PMPs indicates that, on one hand, companies' desperation to find competent managers and, on the other hand, companies' total lack of understanding of the issue. In one sense, it indicates that businesses are at least trying hard to figure out a way to hire competent managers. In comparison, the educational system simply allows teachers to stay there asking for more money, while selling the myth that increasing educational funding is the magic wand to solve all educational problems.

Since it takes one to know one, on a case by case basis, the personnel quality problem has to be solved by someone in the know, but before that, the corporate environment must allow and facilitate those in the know to do the right thing, i.e., for the interests of the company against bureaucratic tendencies. That environment is also known as the realization of the vision thing.

In order to get the vision thing going, leaderships must have some basic characteristics.

First, they need to understand their business. Patton could not have beaten Rommel's Afrika Corps without the thorough understanding of tank warfare and Rommel's tactics. A major part of Jack Welch's success was due to his years of effort to understand GE's myriads of businesses, which was the basis for his implementation of GE's overall vision throughout its business units. Bill Gates et al built Microsoft with their understanding of software and business development. Sam Walton understood everything that was going on in and around Wal-Mart. Alan Greenspan formed his economic opinions based on his understanding of mountains of detailed economic data.

Most company executives are not of that caliber. Those in the know would agree that the most important thing for a successful manager is to understand the unique corporate culture and the particular business environment, and use that understanding in the creative process to improve the existing corporate culture so the company could take advantage of the latest change in the business environment. The existing corporate culture is important because that is a proven way to do business successfully.

PMP's problem, which is also MBA's problem, is to use a generic process to replace all the unique business processes. Skunk works have proved that business specific processes could cost the company only 20 cents on the dollar, which almost always means faster processes. When PMPs push for the idea that people who understand the business specifics should not manage projects, they ask the companies to spend the dollar rather than the 20 cents. The reason behind skunk works is not hard to imagine. If George Patton had not known tank warfare, or Bill Gates had not understood software engineering, they would not be that successful.

A common emphasis of these PMPs is metrics. They have to reduce business practices into numbers so they can use their rules to measure it. Typically, it is easy to measure routine processes, such as a production line, but project management often means managing a project, or the activities of breaking new grounds. Since people do not know where they are going to end up in these creative processes, managing these projects depends mostly on analytical skills. Numerical or statistical measures may be useful but they always serve the analytical aspect. For instance, one may measure completion time-to-estimate ratio. When people working on the project know this, they would try to lengthen their estimates so they can get better numbers. If PMPs do not understand enough business to assess the estimates, the ratio would not mean much.

When Robert McNamara ran Ford Motor Company, he pressed Ford plant managers to produce certain numbers. In order for the numbers to show effectiveness, plant managers threw away spare parts and used empty warehouses to show their effective just-in-time delivery system. The fact is that, if they had enforced just-in-time, they would have to take the risk of shutting down the plants waiting for the delivery of some minor parts.

When John F. Kennedy asked McNamara to run the Department of Defense, he requested the field officers in Vietnam to give him numbers that they could not obtain or were too ashamed to admit, so they fed McNamara cooked data. McNamara and Kennedy Administration made decisions on Vietnam strategies based on those bogus data.

Throughout the Vietnam war, the American government did not have the basic understanding of the business at hand—how to solve the Vietnam problem facing a corrupt South Vietnamese government that did not have the support of the Vietnamese people and a guerrilla force that had the support of the people and was further supported by North Vietnam, the Soviet Union, and China. Before the problems of the South Vietnamese government were solved, there could be no final solution. Throughout the war, Washington was too busy working on the next day's bombing target list to spend time working on the South Vietnamese government.

Management by number without understanding the business itself worked neither at Ford nor in Vietnam.

When one understands details, he could often pick out the data mistakes. For instance, with Greenspan's understanding of economy, he could often identify data errors in reports. On the contrary, without understanding situations at Ford or in Vietnam, McNamara could not identify even obvious data errors in the reports. Not understanding the business at hand and trying to implement some generic system is the fatal shortcoming of the PMPs. By arguing that such understanding is not important, PMPs have demonstrated their ignorance. By allowing PMPs to win such argument, company boards and executives demonstrate their ignorance.

The best way to argue against these PMPs is by borrowing a comment made by Louis Armstrong: "Unless you know what it is, I ain't never going to be able to explain it to you." The test of such understanding is whether they can recognize data errors. In order to pass the test, one has to comprehend the abstraction that covers the company businesses, the company products, and the corporate culture.

The second common characteristic is their innovative and creative abilities to produce a corporate vision. This is beyond what Louis Armstrong talked about. The visions of all great companies, such as Microsoft, Wal-Mart, or McDonald's, are not hard for people to understand, just like Christopher Columbus said once that sailing west was not a hard idea to understand after someone had explained it. McDonald's, in its early days, had a clear vision, which was to provide tasty food fast at low price. As McDonald's customers are more conscious of the health problems caused by greasy burgers, McDonald's needs a new or revised vision to move ahead with its customers. The current executives could not figure out a way for McDonald's to keep the traditional burger eaters happy and appeal to the more health conscious crowd at the same time.

I don't not mean to pick on McDonald's. After Sam Walton, Wal-Mart executives have a hard time to run Wal-Mart in Sam Walton's fashion, although they have kept Sam Walton's tradition of keep trying new things. The problem facing the new generation of managers is that they are not as inquisitive, understanding, and innovative as Sam Walton, leading to Wal-Mart's reduced success rate of its experiments, giving competitors opportunities. McDonald's problem is somewhat the same as Wal-Mart's that, under new environment, the new executives could not repeat what founders have done by keeping the vision moving with the customers and business environment.

The difficulty of innovativeness is for someone to come up with the idea. This is a purely creative endeavor. Visions should not be hard to understand, like Christopher Columbus's sailing west. Good visions are always simple. Normally, convoluted vision is nothing but an indication that the top executives do not know what they are doing. Besides, if a vision is so convoluted that it could not be understood easily by employees from mid-level managers to truck drivers, it has no chance to be implemented.

Under Sam Walton, Wal-Mart kept up with the market by using information technology and economy of scale. Walton made sure that Wal-Mart sold products that the majority of the Americans wanted, in good quality, and at the best price.

After Sam Walton, Wal-Mart started to hire cheap labor to reduce cost. Recently, tired of low margin goods, Wal-Mart executives wanted to enter high-margin designer-clothing market. Since Wal-Mart started to hire the cheapest labor on the market, it has changed its image from selling "high quality everyday goods" to selling "cheap stuff". Now, with dirt cheap sales clerks, one would question how Wal-Mart is going to enter the high-margin product lines that require better quality clerks. In other words, the contradictions prove that the new Wal-Mart executives have a vision problem.

If Wal-Mart executives contradict themselves at such high level, one may expect that Wal-Mart's everyday operational decisions would also be contradictory and self-defeating.

Schools may teach MBAs or PMPs past success stories, but they could not teach the ability to recognize new business environments, the creative and innovative abilities to develop new visions, and the ability to reorganize the organizations continuously to carry out the new visions. Fans of PMPs fail to recognize that PMP certification certifies none of those critical abilities.

The reward for the innovative companies is that, protected by proper measures to keep trade secret (e.g., Coca Cola) and relevant laws, it might take a while for competitors to catch up. Before then, innovative companies could earn an innovative premium. For instance, before companies like Compaq and Dell, IBM made enormous amount of money by selling IBM PCs. In fact, the PC hardware business was so good that IBM did not realize that PC operating system was a market all by itself, and gave the business to Microsoft, an unknown company at the time.

We might view the power of judgment as a special kind of creative power. The difference is that creation concerns producing a new idea, while making judgment concerns evaluating an existing idea. To a company, the judgment ability of the executives is crucial and often more demanding. After all, Sam Walton did not start the idea of mega stores or computer-run distribution systems. Thomas

Jefferson, according to modern academicians, did not create any new ideas. Their value was the ability to determine which idea would work.

The judgment power could also be tested by the ability to see errors in the raw data. The reason is simple. Alan Greenspan could see errors in raw data in the very same way that he could see problems in an untested new idea. Without that ability, people like McNamara make decisions by blindly trying, because even if they were given a good idea, they could not recognize it.

Without visions, executives run the business by random guessing—an extremely inefficient and wasteful undertaking. According to mathematics, the most probable result after many random motions is not moving at all, which is typically what these visionless companies do. Some of them cycle two policies. When Policy A is proven not working, they would implement Policy B, and then when Policy B fails, they would try Policy A again under another name.

The third common characteristic of effective leaders is their abilities to implement a vision, which requires leadership skills. If corporate headquarter has one vision and different business units have their own, it is just as though there is no overall corporate vision at all. The worst situation that I have seen is that CEO could not even get his CTO[1], working next door, to implement his vision.

Once I talked to the CEO of a dot-com, the CEO explained to me that he was trying to establish a business connection between the U.S. and the Far East, particularly China. In fact, the company had successfully helped a Chinese client purchase a PC network by conducting an online auction involving all major U.S. PC makers, saving the Chinese client a lot of money. He expressed the wish to focus the company on the core businesses, but when I talked to the CTO, he told me that he was in the process of spending tens of millions of dollars establishing a whole internet environment with search engines and news, all with purchased technologies. When CEO's vision could not even get through to his CTO, I could only wonder whose vision the lower tier managers would implement.

Implementing a vision throughout an organization requires leadership skills. This is also one of those situations that it takes one to know one. For those without leadership experience, it is difficult to understand how leadership works and why it could be so effective, to the point that they do not believe the existence of effective leadership. For instance, today, academicians began to second-guess the leadership skills of George Patton in North Africa in March 1943, by arguing

---

1.   Chief Technologies Officer

that Patton could not have made that big a difference between March 6 when he took over the command of the II Corp from Lloyd Fredendall and March 23 when he turned back the German 10th Panzer Division at El Guettar, although nobody suggested that Fredendall could have done the same. The second-guessers ignored the spirit that Patton brought to the II Corp, which was best described by himself to his officers before El Guettar: "Gentlemen, tomorrow we attack. If we are not victorious, let no man come back alive." Without that spirit, Fredendall nearly allowed Rommel's panzers to destroy the II Corp at Kasserine Pass; with that spirit, Patton prevailed at El Guettar.

It is no wonder that the doubts come from today's academicians, who believe that people could not be changed, especially in a short time. If they admit that George Patton had converted so many defeatists into fanatics in less than three weeks, they have to admit that they do not deserve their paycheck ultimately from the taxpayers, for not converting defeatist students into learning fanatics, so the sensible thing for them to do is to explain that some unknown natural event—but not Patton's leadership skills—somehow changed the II Corp.

One way to evaluate a company's implementation ability is by observing the equilibrium point between the force of change and the force of bureaucratic resistance.

For instance, once, Disney decided to cut its workforce. In order to reduce the difficulties of the task, the middle management encouraged people to leave voluntarily, promising them the same severance package, not worrying that competent people were more likely to take advantage of the package. ARCO[2] management did better because it required management approval for the volunteers to receive severance pay when it had to lay off people.

Both Disney and ARCO were good companies. In other companies, the situation could be much worse. Once, I had a consulting job in a company that is listed at NASDAQ with capitalization of more than $700M. The management of MIS[3] department had no idea what was going on and had no set strategy to handle problems. Consequently, the MIS department resembled a mad house. Every single day, there were urgent problems. Everyone was tasked to solve those particular problems. As soon as the problems were solved, people forgot about the underlying causes right away, because they needed a break, until the underlying causes created another set of problems the next day. Patchwork was constantly

2.   Atlantic Richfield Company has been purchased by British Petroleum.
3.   Management Information Services

undergoing by a consulting company attempting to fix a fundamentally poor design. The attention span of the manager was so short that I could not hold a conversation with him for more than a couple of minutes. When I proposed a solution to him, he wanted to see something "working" in two weeks. As I started to explain to him that, like building a house, we needed a design before sending in concrete trucks, he told me that planning was "fluff" work and moved his attention elsewhere.

The history with this company is that the manager asked a consulting firm to come up with something quick. The consulting company dutifully agreed. With a design that any adequately trained computer science professional would cry foul, the system was completed in one year, which took another two years of stabilizing work to make it usable. The problem is that the company was in the buying mode. It needed a flexible system to merge more than 40 companies, all using different systems.

The CIO, his boss, told me that he just wanted things to be done right, but didn't care how. In his words, he wanted the IT system to work like telephone: "When you pick up a phone, you always expect a dial tone."

In the age of information technologies, this company had employees dedicated to the task of copying. Every week, it sent out truck full of paper that was to be shipped around the world via FedEx. A primitive information system costing $50,000 could easily save the company millions of dollars a year. (Since the company did mostly government contract, it probably did not care about such expenses.)

During the discussions before I started consulting for the company, the MIS manager promised me that I would work closely with the CIO and the CEO to establish a new system to integrate the information systems of different business units. I never met the CEO and talked to the CIO only a couple of times. Each time, the meeting lasted for no more than a couple of minutes. I got nothing but nonsense from the CIO such as the telephone analogy. With such grand act of ignorance by the leadership of the company, what would they expect at the bottom?

When working with other high-tech firms, I was never the most health conscious person in the group, but with this company, I was by far the healthiest, as others drank heavily, over-ate, smoked, drank coffee continuously, and did not exercise. I personally felt like a stranger there.

I made a proposal that would take a year to overhaul the system with the first deliverable in 6 months. The consultant flew in for a couple of days. My consultancy was quickly and mercifully terminated.

That is not the worst that I have seen. Once, I was interviewed by an executive of a dot-com company. After I told the hiring manager that I was looking for a management type position, he told me that he had enough chiefs but no Indians. I instinctively told him, "No, your problem is that you have no chief." I got nowhere with the company, and the company got nowhere in the marketplace.

At another dot-com, I found that all programmers were working in a hacker mentality. There was no overall understanding or strategy of the project. When I insisted to the management that development without any documentation did not stand a chance to succeed, they terminated my consulting contract. The interesting thing I heard was that, after I was gone, every programmer was told to write documentation, as if getting programmers to write documentation would make them understand where they were going and how. I could only laugh when hearing this. These managers did not even know that documentation was merely a tool to serve a purpose. It was not an end to itself.

At the same company, I remember talking to one of the founders over lunch about the need to take care of the competent programmers. He dismissed my idea with a wave of his hand, "Nah, programmers are dime a dozen."

Needless to say, those dot-com companies did not last long as they burned through investor's money like a wild fire.

It is the duty of the top management to make sure that middle management carries out company's vision. One popular problem with the top management is that they spend too little time with the operations of the company, including COOs who are supposed to do nothing but taking care of the operations of the company. The result is that there is a nicely written vision and there is an operation that has nothing to do with it whatsoever. To judge a company's ability to implement its vision, one only needs to ask different employees to explain the vision in their own words. If they could not do that, the vision itself has never been implemented.

In bad companies, with poor ability to implement the vision, the equilibrium point tilts toward the bureaucratic middle management, which makes the company resemble the educational system that make decisions according to teacher's convenience rather than for the purpose of educating the students.

Some say that managers are manipulators. That could be a true statement in either case, because people could say that Patton manipulated the II Corp. When management manages by lying, the organization would be in a very sorry state. When I worked for Fujifilm, the director of my department told me something I liked to hear. As a piece of good news, I told my boss. He smiled and said, "And you believe that?" It turned out that my boss was right.

The fourth common characteristic of effective leaders is that, besides the insatiable desire to take care of their customers, they take care of their employees.

In bad companies, employees are abused, normally by incompetent managers. A friend of mine once worked for an import-export company. He told me that he was required to report to work at 9 a.m., but typically got his first batch of work right before lunch and second right before the time for him to go home. He said that the boss did this intentionally. Even if my friend was wrong, the boss failed to use his employee's time effectively.

Another friend worked for an attorney. He told me that the attorney spent a lot of time on the phone or out of office, so he had to wait around a lot during the day time. The lawyer seemed to start to think what he should do for that day right around 5 p.m.

The only way to solve those problems is by finding another job.

Many companies like to use the phrase "corporate family", hinting that they treat their employees as family members. I have seen companies that actually do this. Once, I visited a hospital in Michigan, and was amazed at the fact that almost everyone had worked there for more than 20 years. After learning that they were paid at or slightly below industry average, I asked their manager how he did it. He smiled and said, "You treat them right."

Trust is a necessary component of being a family. Most companies fail to do what they say. For example, many U.S. West retirees had been happily holding on to the U.S. West stocks and making decent livings on dividends. After Quest, one of those Wall Street-made darlings that nobody had heard of before, merged with U.S. West, with one announcement, $2.14/share annual dividend was reduced to $0.05. At the same time, the stock started plummeting. Many former U.S. West employees had the bulk of their investment in U.S. West stocks and depended on the dividends to support their lifestyle. Overnight, they had to adjust their lifestyle because their dividend income was no longer there. It probably meant little to tell them that they were more fortunate than those holding WorldCom stocks.

Before BP bought ARCO, ARCO could be called a family oriented company. Many people had worked there for decades, betting on the prospect that ARCO would take care of them. After the BP takeover, BP people (mostly former Amoco people) came in with Al Dunlap's playbook and outsourced the entire IT department to a low bidder. All ARCO employees had to choose from working for the low bidder or leaving. Interestingly, after masterful BP hands finished their jobs, previously half-full main inside parking lot of the ARCO Los Angeles Refinery became constantly full. (By the way, their mentor Dunlap recently settled an SEC civil lawsuit, accusing him of filing false and misleading financial reports for Sunbeam between 1996 and 1998, by paying $500,000.)

In other words, one should always take company's promise with a grain of salt. Even a company that treats its employees nicely and has all intentions to continue its practice may change its mind by a whim due to the other need such as selling the company at a price that is too good for the board to say no. The problem is that, while the company thinks that it is expressing a good faith intention, its employees think that they are getting a promise. For instance, compared to other oil giants, ARCO had a disproportionably large upstream operation[4], so crude price on the world market influenced ARCO more than others. When the oil price was at the lowest point in decades, ARCO's evaluation would be at its lowest point. When oil price subsequently rose, ARCO would be worth more and more. Since ARCO sold itself to BP at the lowest point of the oil price, it made a disservice to its share-holders, as well as its employees.

In other words, if a company does not have the ability to take care of itself, it could not take care of the employees even if it wants to.

Today's companies have another side that people do not normally see. It seriously went wrong at the end of the last economic boom. We are, of course, talking about the accounting and finance side of the operation.

Today, large companies do not do their accounting on cash basis[5]. When they sell something, they record income as account receivable before receiving payment. In the future, when they fail to collect, they would write that off in a later SEC filing.

The benefit of such accounting is that the balance sheet of each quarter reflects more on what companies have done in that quarter, but it gives companies chances to manipulate their books. For instance, when a company is not doing well, they would give deep discount for clients to sign up before the end of the quarter, so they may improve their quarterly figures. (This activity, although odd as the accounting departments run the operation of the companies, has always been legal.)

---

4.   "Upstream" is an oil lingo indicating operations such as exploration and drilling. In other words, ARCO's cost for crude is fixed with its upstream expenses, while other companies buy more oil from open market. The benefit is that, when oil price shot up later, ARCO would make nice profit for BP.

5.   It means that income is recorded only when cash is received.

Without money in the bank as an ultimate check, companies have many ways to cook their books. For instance, they could do circular trade with another company. In other words, Company A could sell things to Company B and Company B could sell it back to Company A. At the end of the dot-com run, when people focused on the amount of business a company had done, rather than earning, to determine the stock price, this was helpful because, with the trade, both Company A and Company B could record sales, although no earning was generated.

In the WorldCom case, financial people simply wrote $500 millions earning in the accounting system without any backup data. It is much easier to make an entry of $500 millions than actually going out there and making it in the real world.

When companies promote CFOs to CEO positions, I always pay a little more attention to the vision of companies. That habit started when I was at the University of Virginia. At several accounting school seminars, people from large companies including IBM[6] stated that accounting and finance professionals had an excellent chance to reach CEO positions. At that time, I could not fathom how American companies could be so great when they were run by bean counters. The answer came some years later when I discovered that those were not great companies.

For public companies, shareholder approval is a quantitative thing, i.e., the stock price. The purpose for all those accounting maneuvers is to promote stock price, but these accounting maneuvers often cost companies a lot of money as they have to hire accounting and legal experts to cook the books. None of such maneuvers actually makes money except indirect benefits such as better credit rating (i.e., easier access to loans and lower interest rate).

That opens another can of worms, as many in Wall Street do not think that they are in a service industry connecting investors and companies. They consider that everyone in the nation ultimately work for them.

During the dot-com boom, as investors started to buy companies that had never made a penny, Wall Street got to decide which startup to go public, making it the Wild Wild West. In Los Angeles, there were people driving Ferraris, going in an out of expensive clubs, claiming that they had Wall Street connection to the dot-com wannabes. They typically would charge $6,000 and 6-8% of the startup fund for their service. I tried to investigate the background of one of these "venture experts" and failed to find any connection between him and Wall Street.

---

6.   The statement was made around 1990, before Louis Gerstner took over.

Industry heavyweights do not play the Ferraris-country club game. One of their games is the evaluation or rating game. For instance, Wall Street heavy-weight (i.e., investment banks such as Salomon Smith Barney and analysts such as Jack Grubman) identified these aggressive new companies (e.g., WorldCom, Enron, and Global Crossing), and boosted their images by high ratings and sup-portive reports, which brought investors' support and allowed the companies to buy their way into eminence through incurring unreasonable debts. In the mean-time, investment banks and specialists would make billions in fees.

When Grubman was finally called to testify in Congress, he mentioned the Chinese wall. Under that arrangement, when Grubman was called to service Salomon's banking clients (i.e., companies) in business activities such as stock issuances or M&A[7], he would remain on the banking side (i.e., the company side) of the Chinese wall until the proprietary information was made public before returning to his analyst role (i.e., the investor side). Even to a financial lay person, the obvious conflict of interests makes the so-called Chinese wall a joke.

When Grubman helped Bernie Ebbers of WorldCom—a company that came to scene from nowhere—to buy MCI, the offer price was so high that MCI could not say no, but the WorldCom investors started to worry that they had paid too much, causing WorldCom's stock price to fall. Seeing the problem, Grubman immediately climbed to the other side of the Chinese wall and wrote glamorous commentaries about WorldCom. WorldCom's stock price recovered. For the next six months, WorldCom stock hit $60 before it started the dive to $0.06 and was de-listed by NASDAQ. A critical part of WorldCom's successful acquisition of MCI was Grubman's ability to rally investors' support with his reviews, but his real interests were for the M&A to take place so his company, Salomon Smith Barney, as the underwriting bank, could make millions in fees. The future of WorldCom, which was overburdened by debt, and the interests of the investors, who bought either WorldCom's stocks or bonds, were not his concern. For his trouble of intentionally sacrificing those who trusted him, Salomon paid Grub-man $20 million a year. From the telecommunication industry alone, Salomon made almost $1 billion for underwriting securities and providing advices to tele-comm companies between 1997 and 2002, according to Thomson Financial[8]. That money had to come from somewhere.

---

7.   Mergers and acquisitions
8.   http://www.thestreet.com/markets/kristenfrench/10019951.html (11/9/2002)

With IPO[9] fees at 6-7% of the total offering, gaining companies as clients or manufacturing IPOs and M&As was the name of the game for investment banks. When Internet companies that had never made a penny could launch successful IPOs, influence was the name of the game. Investment banks needed these analysts who could write influential reports so they could launch successful IPOs. Analysts like Grubman played the role of dressing up a pig as a darling and selling it to the public. At the peak of the dot-com days, they robbed both the honest companies and the investors. (When investment banks knew that the stock prices would go through the roof in the first day, the banks should have priced the IPO much higher, so the company could get more cash, which was the purpose of public offering and what the underwriting banks were paid to do. The investment banks priced stocks low and sold them to their potential banking customers as legal bribery and a way to create public euphoria. When the price finally collapsed, analysts did not downgrade these companies until the stocks were almost worthless, making the trusting public the last to get out.) In the process, the Wall Street professionals took care of the players. For instance, when ImClone was in trouble, Martha Steward got to dump her shares before everyone else.

The practice of Wall Street firms publishing their rating itself is a scam and should be banned, because at minimum they know their rating change before others, giving them an unfair edge to act before others.

Grubman blamed his failure to predict the collapse of the telecomm companies on bad information from the companies—"garbage-in-garbage-out," as he put it, which was outright spinning, because he knew what he was doing when he climbed through the Chinese wall to keep WorldCom's stock from falling.

He was right on one point. As SEC allows wide variety of accounting practices, "garbage-in-garbage-out" could happen quite easily for an investor. Even under Sarbanes-Oxley, SEC is authorized to "recognize, as 'generally accepted'…any accounting principles"[10]. For investors, arguably the most useful value of accounting report is the validity of comparing the numbers, e.g., PE[11] ratio, of one company with another.

Sarbanes-Oxley increased companies' reporting responsibilities but did not lock all companies, at least industry by industry, into a uniform accounting principle, rather than "generally accepted" accounting principles. As different compa-

---

9.   Initial Public Offering
10. Section 108 of Sarbanes-Oxley Act of 2002
11. Stock price-to-earning ratio equals to the number of years for investors to make the money back under the current rate.

nies choose to use different "generally accepted" accounting principles, their final numbers mean different things. Comparing one company's PE against the other becomes foolhardy.

Financial professionals are against a uniform accounting principle, because it would rid them of their values. Within the accounting profession, there is this joke that a company was looking for a CFO. When the first candidate walked into the door, the CEO handed him a sheet of paper with financial numbers on it and asked whether the company had made money. After some calculation, the candidate said, "Yes, the company made money." He was told to leave. When the next candidate came in, he was handed the same sheet of paper. After his calculation, he said, "No, the company lost money." He was told to leave too. When the third candidate was handed the paper, he read it for a moment and asked, "Do you want the company to make money or lose money?" He was hired.

The question for CEOs is whether to report numbers as they are or spend real money to manipulate the numbers to make their books look better. Many CEOs opt to spend the money.

Playing games with GAAP[12] is not as hard as some might think. For instance, companies could choose to use FIFO[13] or LIFO[14] as accounting basis (independent of their shipment of real goods). The different selections may make a difference in the financial numbers. As another example, GAAP allows the companies to decide whether to amortize a certain expense. In order to make the books look better, companies categorize outright cost of doing business as capital expenditure and amortize it.

One problem with GAAP is that it is maintained by FASB[15], which is influenced heavily by the accounting profession, but we are getting beyond the scope of this book.

The GAAP game boosts the importance of CFOs, as companies need them to dress up their financial reports. Many CFOs are promoted to be CEOs.

The most inexcusable aspect of the game is that it confuses amateur investors who do not have time to either read the fine print of the financial reports or comb through the numbers looking for inconsistencies, although many professional investors who are either too lazy to form their independent opinions or too feeble to stand up against such legal manipulations for the sole purpose of misleading the public. People in the profession, including financial reporters, would not cry

---

12.   Generally Accepted Accounting Practices
13.   First-in-first-out
14.   Last-in-first-out
15.   The Financial Accounting Standards Board

foul when they see problems because they don't want to rain on the parade and make enemies. For instance, the dot-com problems were recognized by many people for a long time, but nobody reported it before the collapse.

Alan Greenspan warned "irrational exuberance" in December 1996[16], commenting that it could cause "unexpected and prolonged contractions as they have in Japan over the past decade". It made the front page news because Greenspan broke the rule of not commenting on stock prices, but with everyone else remaining mute, he did not deter investors. Collapse came more than three years later in 2000.

It was Prisoner's Dilemma at work. For those who understood what was going on, it was more important for them to make some money at the cost of the nation's future as a whole. Many Wall Street players understood Greenspan's comment, but they chose not to acknowledge it because ignoring it could bring billions to them; and they were not about to let that golden opportunity go.

At the time of finalizing this book in 2006, the U.S. is still recovering from long technological winter that started in 2000. Since much of the technical work has been outsourced to India, China, etc., the old days might never come back. Also, although there are signs that companies are finishing up licking their wound, many are still holding back their development projects.

As wealth spread, the efficient use of smaller investors' money becomes increasingly important to the economy. Small investors have to deal with retail brokers, who tend to serve their own interests rather than the interests of the investors. Their principle is "If you have it, sell it; if you don't have it, buy it." Such practice is caused by the fact that if a broker buys a great stock for his clients, the clients would make a lot of money by holding on to the stock as the stock goes up, but the broker is going to make nothing in the process, because he only makes money when transactions take place. Mutual funds are created to solve the problem because brokers can continuously take money from the investors in the name of active management, in express as well as hidden fees. Most mutual funds don't even match the performance of the index. In order words, they are nothing but schemes for brokers to pocket investors' money.

When investors complain to brokers for their failure to protect invested funds, brokers would put up lame excuses.

---

16.   Speech at the Annual Dinner and Francis Boyer Lecture of The American Enterprise Institute for Public Policy Research, Washington, D.C., December 5, 1996

"The market is going down, so your account value is going down," ignoring the fact they are paid to prevent that from happening.

"Just hold on to the stocks. The price would come back up." Tell that to the holders of Global Crossing or WorldCom stocks.

"Over the long run, stock market provides the best returns." The fact is that when the value drops 50%, the market has to go up 100% for the investor to recoup the loss. If an investor was involved in WorldCom and got out late, say after losing 99% of the value, the market had to rise 10,000% for the investor to break even, which is the day when NASDAQ hits 200,000.

Some of the lies are quite hideous. Once, a broker tried to convince me to buy some recallable bonds in 2002. It was a 15-year bond, recallable in five years. He nonchalantly told me that the company probably would recall the bond in five years. Considering the low interest rate in 2002, it was a good deal if I counted on the company to recall in five years. In fact, a friend of mine was interested in buying the bond. I told him that the 5-year recallable term killed his upside, which was the unlikely event of even lower interest rate. If the interest rate went up, which was likely in five years, the issuer would not recall; and the bondholders were stuck with the low interest rate bond for the whole 15 years. If the interest rate went down, the company would recall it in five years and deny the investors that additional percent or two. Certainly, the broker violated no laws by dropping hints so the investors would calculate on the assumption of five-year recall, but as my friend understood the situation, he gave up the idea of buying that bond immediately.

When people rob banks, there is only limited amount of money that they can get with enormous risks. They have to use guns and know that police are not going to hesitate to take a shot at them. But when people make misleading recommendations, lie on their books, trade with insider information, or distribute intentionally under priced, thus hot, IPO stocks as legal bribes to potential clients, they rob the public at almost no risk.

Today, many privately-owned companies under competent leadership choose not to go public because they don't want to put their fate in the hands of Wall Street whose morality is questionable at best and their pursuit of quarterly report would lead to bad business decisions. They would rather stay small and focus on their customers and employees. Allowing these companies to expand is the duty of Wall Street. As excellent companies refuse to go public, Wall Street forfeits its responsibilities and impedes the progress of the U.S. economy.

But, generally speaking, when compared to other systems in the U.S. , the business system is healthiest. Applying Newton's laws again, in the business system, customers' pull is their power to choose among competitors. They choose the company that provides the best service with the lowest price, requiring the successful companies to understand-innovate-implement and be efficient. Company's pull is their advertising campaign, but unsuccessful companies are at a competitive disadvantage of advertising dollars because truth would get out sooner or later and advertising alone won't change that.

Shareholders are also supposed to pull the companies toward the customers' side, because happy customers are the only assurance for shareholders' highest return of their investment. Although companies could manipulate their books, they could not cook their bank accounts for ever. In other words, cooking books is only a short term solution. Sooner or later, though bank accounts, investors would realize that the company is in a hole and the executives are digging deeper and deeper by further manipulations. A quick look at the balance sheet could give investors a rough idea of the cash position versus debt. From that point, it is easy to do further researches of the liabilities.

Not all investment mistakes are caused by systematic problems. Investment is, by its nature, a risk-taking action. Ted Turner was a good risk taker when he invested in TBS and CNN, but when he pushed Time Warner to invest in AOL by merging with the ISP[17], he was, once again, knowingly taking a big risk because many people have told him that. One may always argue that Turner was over his head to deal with new technologies and allowed the Internet hoopla to overwhelm his cool-headed business calculation, but that should not be considered a systematic problem. On the contrary, allowing investors to try different things is precisely what makes an effective and efficient system that, over all, uses money most effectively and efficiently.

All in good time, bad companies, no matter how skillful and creative their accounting people are, would have cash shortages to pay their obligations. They would have to shortchange their customers in research and development of new products, advertising, and post-sales services in order to cover their debts. It is the time that investors should realize that something is wrong. Under some circumstances, Sarbanes-Oxley could send the executives to jail.

Although accounting experts are still burning their midnight oil to use "generally accepted accounting principles" to work around Sarbanes-Oxley, and the stock prices, especially that of technologies stocks, are still depressed, the innova-

---

17.   Internet Service Provider that gives users entrance points to the Internet.

tive nature of the American businesses should be able to pull the U.S. financial market out of the current hole. It is not likely for us to see wholesale problems in the U.S. in the scale of Korea or China. In other words, it is not likely that we will see the so-called Korean Discount[18] in the U.S. market.

In the long run, the only thing that macroscopically discounts the U.S. stock price is the lack of competency of the corporate executive and managers who could not understand-innovate-implement new business endeavors. The best place to start solving that problem, of course, is the educational system. Since we are not going to see fundamental reform of the educational system as long as the *de facto* monopoly is in place, corporations have to find/discover/train one executive/manager/employee at a time.

Also, business people often have subconscious filter problem. For instance, a Los Angeles law firm advertised heavily in the Chinese language media, generating many telephone inquiries, but it kept hiring $8-to-$12 an hour receptionist/paralegal/office-manager to talk to these potential clients, because of the belief that Chinese labor was cheap. Rarely any client signed up with the firm, so they complained that the Chinese clients were seeking cheaper lawyers, failing to explain why these callers often ended up hiring someone more expensive. Companies are as strong as its weakest link. For this LA law firm, the weakest link is the person who answers the phone.

This L.A. law firm was especially bad at this as the managing attorneys continued to believe that the problem was with their clients but not their approach. To solve the problem, it moved into a more expensive building to impress its potential clients, but still advertised for an all-around person expressly at $8 to $12 an hour.

---

18. In international investment, Korean shares are cheap relative to other Asian markets. The phenomenon is known as Korean Discount. One explanation is the lack of corporate ethics in Korea. For instance, in the past couple of years, top officials of Samsung Electronics, Hyundai Motor, and Korean Air have faced jail sentences. The demise of Korean powerhouse Daewoo is another example.

7

The Economic System

Neither the educational system nor the business system has changed fundamentally in the past 100 years, which seems to support the cultural cliché that it is impossible to change the collective subconscious filters of individuals as well as societies.

The sea changes of the economic system in the past couple of centuries stand out as the contrary example as the prevailing economic philosophy changed twice. First, it changed from *lassie-faire* colonial global economy to government-controlled economy. Second, powerful reforms carried out by several determined politicians stopped the idea of government-run economy cold turkey, and drove the world into a global market economy.

The changes took different forms in different countries. For Britain and the U.S., the exploiting monopolistic capitalists brought the first turn; and the inept governments the second. In Russia, the first turn came when the Bolsheviks stole the revolution triggered by the prolonged and meaningless European wars, and the second with the economic collapse of the Soviet Union. In China, the first turn was triggered by the hyperinflation and the widespread corruption of Jiang Jieshi[1]'s nationalist government. Deng Xiaoping brought the second turn after Mao Zedong's death. Japan hit the bottom for the first time after WWII, when people would literally kill each other for one U.S. dollar. Douglas MacArthur bought the first change to Japan. So far, the Japanese government and the industrial *keiretsu*[2] have been resisting the second turn.

In business (a.k.a. microeconomics), people see what is happening right in front of their eyes. When a broker asks his client to buy a stock that tanks, the cli-

---

1. His name is also translated as Chiang Kai-shek
2. Keiretsu is a network of businesses that own stakes in one another as a means of mutual security. Members usually include large manufacturers, their suppliers, and banks.

ent knows that he has just made a wrong move. When a company goes on a shopping spree and does not seem to have the ability to digest the newly acquired business units, one wonders how it is going to deal with the mounting debt. When a company loses business to competitors quarter after quarter, everybody knows that something is wrong.

Economy (a.k.a. macroeconomics) is different because of its higher level of abstraction. Understanding of the high-level abstraction is required to see what is happening. Economic policies do not deal with anyone in particular but deal with everyone in general. When the economy is in trouble, it is quite possible that public won't be able to figure out what is wrong. For instance, when government-controlled economy runs into trouble, people might support the policy for government to apply more control to concentrate investment and eliminate unpredictability. (It happened in the Nixon Administration.) In addition, it takes time for the effects of economic policies to become evident. (Jimmy Carter started to tighten the money supply by appointing Paul Volcker to chair the Federal Reserve Board, but did not see much improvement in his term.)

In agrarian societies, where people are self-sufficient, they may ignore government policies and make their own livings by planting their own food and weaving their own cloth, but those societies are destroyed irreversibly by the efficiency of the global division of labor. Today, we are the slaves of the macroeconomic environment and government economic policies. For instance, when the market economy runs into soft spots, people stop buying, forcing good companies to stop producing and lay quality people off, triggering further reduction in buying power, thus further layoffs. The vicious cycle forces people out of work. At that point, able and willing people are denied opportunities to work and make a living. If the economic trouble coincides with high inflation, the candle burns at both ends as jobless people see their savings evaporating quickly.

One hundred years after the U.S. independence, Britain still ran a global economy with a network covering much of the world. It won the world over by ideas, including *lassie-faire* economics and free trade. In the period of global economic boom, which is known as mercantilism, free trade fueled the economy, which allowed the living standard to rise rapidly throughout the network. The natives in colonies were fascinated by the changes that Britain brought to them, and gave Britain the administrative control. Since Britain got the hearts and souls of the natives, a weak administrative and military presence was sufficient for Britain to run the enormous empire.

Militarily, Britain was so weak that it could not suppress rebellions even when colonies rebelled one at a time. For example, its professional soldiers failed to destroy George Washington's Continental Army. For some reason, Britain did not realize that its attempt to implement administrative (tax) and military (Lexington and Concord) control was the cause of the American rebellion. It went ahead to do the same to its other colonies, which put Britain in a vicious cycle: First, it implemented more administrative control; second, it needed money to cover the cost; third, London was forced to increase local tax; forth, higher tax created resentment; fifth, to handle resentment, London needed more control and more muscle. Since Britain taxed trade, it damaged its very charm—its *raison d'être*—in the eyes of the natives. Like all other declining super powers, Britain failed to reach a higher abstraction when facing problems and responded to problems with self-destructive policies.

After giving birth and death of mercantilism, Britain gave birth to the government-controlled economy. After all, Karl Marx wrote his *Das Kapital* mostly in the British Library's Reading Room in London. John Maynard Keynes, Britain's native son, came up with his complete system of government-run economy, when he published his *General Theory of Employment, Income and Rate of Interest* in 1936. We might say that Western socialism was the mixture of Marx and Keynes, while the Eastern socialism (according to Marx's definition), known in the West as communism, was the mixture of Marx and Vladimir Ilyich Lenin, with Marx as the common theoretical root.

If imitation is the highest form of infatuation, Britain could be proud to have the hearts of its former colonies in the move toward government control. In fact, in one degree or another, the whole world went socialism as governments throughout the world took over the responsibility of distributing resources and labor "rationally", resulting in ever increasing budget deficit and inflation.

The climax of the shift to government control was reached at the end of WWII, when Clement Atlee soundly defeated Winston Churchill in 1945. Churchill's defeat was not a mysterious event, as some suggested after the defeat of George Bush, Sr. in 1992. Churchill campaigned on the principle that the government was the problem rather than the solution. He even went so far to compare the British government to the Gestapo and promised to adopt Hayek's economic ideals. The British people could not understand how the British government that had just led them to victory over the Gestapo could be the problems, let alone being the Gestapo. Atlee further took advantage of the British xenophobia by denouncing Churchill of promoting the idea of a foreigner.

Whenever mentioning Hayek, Atlee would use his full name—Friedrich August von Hayek. In this ill-informed vote, contradictions were all over the places. The British people turned their back on Churchill who had just led them to victory in WWII, opted for a government-run economic system that was only fully tested by Lenin and Hitler, and gave their trust to an unknown figure (i.e., Atlee) to carry it out. Nobody mentioned that Hitler's socialist system could not run for long before a war was necessary, while the evils of Lenin's system were already apparent in 1945. With Atlee's brilliant cunning job, and Churchill's lack of campaign acumen, those issues were never fully debated.

The sad part of the story is that even if those issues had been properly raised and fairly debated, Churchill probably would still have lost because big-government theories had gained the support of the people.

John F. Kennedy, when receiving an honorary degree from Yale, said, "What is at stake in our economic decisions today is not some grand warfare of rival ideology, which will sweep the country with passion, but the practical management of a modern economy. What we need is not labels and clichés, but more basic discussion of the sophisticated and technical questions involved in keeping a great economic machinery moving ahead."[3] So, the question was no longer whether the government should control the economy but how it could do it better—a point that is still held by many academicians today.

With hindsight, we now know that the government control is destined to disaster. To make the government-controlled system work, bureaucrats must have the full control of the economic activities of the nation, and completely take out the disruptions of the market force, which is caused by customers' demands and businesses' innovations that meet or create the demands. In other words, the government has to deny the creativeness and individualities of everyone in the nation to make their plans valid in the first place.

With control, the human nature of those bureaucrats would drive them to grab more power, which further takes away the decision-making power from the people. Initially, people in government still remember the purpose of government control. Soon, especially after the first generation leaders retire, control becomes the end as well as the means.

For small countries like Cuba, despite disastrous, the system of total control might last because the government could deal with matters on a case-by-case basis, but for a nation as big as the Soviet Union and China, the idea of total con-

---

3.   http://www.cs.umb.edu/jfklibrary/j061162.htm (9/12/2002)

trol is absurd. It is relatively more practical for government to run the economy via private ownership and government regulations, as Britain and the U.S. did.

In Britain and the U.S. , when the government proudly played the role of Robin Hood, unions gained immediate power. Management quickly came to the realization that the best way for it to play the game was to grant the unions whatever they wanted and simply passed on the cost to the customers. Labor unions went wild pushing for benefits. Economically, that situation was equivalent to a tax. With union monopoly, the tax grew rapidly. For instance, the Big Three automakers in Detroit gave their unions whatever they asked for, by simply jacking up the prices of the cars, stopping innovating, and turning a deaf ear to the quality problems. The party lasted until Japanese automakers came in and took a big chunk of market from the Big Three.

Inflation is the result of irresponsible government spending. Through inflation, the government steals money from the people by reducing the value of the money in their hands. In fact, many people knew the evils of inflation and made effort to prevent it. As chancellor of Exchequer, Churchill tried to tie the Pound Sterling to gold. The U.S. government agreed in 1944, at the Bretton Woods Conference, to keep the price of gold at $35 an ounce. That, of course, was mere fancy. Nixon finally abandoned Bretton Woods and allowed the gold price to float according to market supply and demand.

Since bureaucrats don't have to make money in the first place like everyone else, they spend it mindlessly at an ever increasing pace like any bad addiction. The efficiency of money decreases correspondingly. Gradually, the government would burn money for no good reason. Sooner or later, the government could no longer raise the spending level by taxation and inflation, because the economy is on the line. That is the so-called stagflation—economic stagnation with high inflation—impossible according to Keynes' General Theories.

In a business sense, at best, it is a case of privileges without obligations. At worst, this is one of the oldest cons—you give the victim $1 and take $10 from him with the promise of $100, which would, of course, never come. Government spending becomes an addiction for politicians. For a long time, even reducing the rate of increase would make the politicians cry foul.

It took a long time for people to understand Churchill and realize the nature of government control. Prior to that realization, people believed that under government control, they would never see unemployment, exploitation, and uncertainty. All they had to suffer was mild inflation. Although Keynesians might not admit it, they based their propaganda primarily on Marxist class-warfare theories by declaring to the people that the government was on their side, fighting against the evil employers who were out there to exploit everyone.

Richard Nixon entered the White House with high hopes of the free marketers as he employed many University of Chicago economists including George Shultz (OMB Director) and Milton Friedman (economic adviser), but down below, Nixon was an economic opportunist. When inflation and unemployment problems became acute, Nixon opted for price and wage controls[4]. The political reality was that, if Nixon had set out to slay the "inflation dragon", George McGovern might have slain him in 1972. As it turned out, Nixon won his reelection by 49 states and gave McGovern only Massachusetts and District of Columbia. Since it took time for his economic policies to show their full effect, Jimmy Carter was left to carry the Nixon baggage and got almost no credit for his effort of slaying the inflation dragon. Most of the work was done in Reagan's first term a decade after Nixon.

The power of economic policies is enormous. Under Nixon's price control, price was set lower than the production cost, so instead of limiting inflation, the policy shut down productions, creating more unemployment, and driving the inflation even higher with less tax income for the government.

The Marxist-Leninist system was a tragedy from the onset. Even Lenin realized that his "red terror" would not work economically. Against strong Party opposition, he went ahead with his New Economic Policy by giving up direct government control of peasant and petty bourgeois. Stalin would have none of it. He implemented extensive collectivism and focused on the industrial growth, especially that of heavy industry. His magic wand was to produce massive number of "enemies of the people" to be used as forced labors.

Although Russian people openly belittled the communist economic policies in the 1950s, nobody stood up to protest in public. After Nikita Khrushchev, no intelligent Russian people bought the economic policies of the string of Soviet bureaucrats, including Mikhail Gorbachev.

Mao Zedong did not have the guts to be that brutal. Instead, he launched one "political movement" after another. Of course, the massive government-orga-

---

4.   To bring down inflation, the government has to tighten the money supply, which increases interest rate. High interest rate would induce economic contraction because companies could afford less money. Contraction always increase unemployment rate. When the economy already suffers both high inflation and high unemployment rate, there is no painless way to get out of the vicious cycle.

nized nonsense could not possibly have produced the economic miracle that Mao had expected. The most notorious of his economic efforts was the so-called Giant Leap Forward Movement in 1958, which nearly destroyed the Chinese economy. Out of respect for him, the politburo let Mao Zedong keep his Party chairman's title. Before using the Cultural Revolution to get the power back, Mao Zedong essentially retired. For a while, he did not even attend the politburo meetings.

Hayek described the problem brilliantly in his bestselling book *The Road to Serfdom*. The center of his argument was that, when the government took over control, people were rendered slaves, without the freedom to determine their own fate.

One might say that the first antidote to the Marxism-Keynesianism was offered by Germany, but just as nobody wanted to talk about Autobahn, nobody wanted to talk about Ludwig Erhard. When appointed Director of the Administration for Economics in 1948, Erhard single-handedly, without consulting anyone, went on the radio and abandoned all price controls—a primal example of shock therapy. That single-handed move was responsible for putting the German economy ahead of the British economy.

The first sign of the global turn toward market economy came as an accident. In the 1970s, Hayek was so lonely that he said that he was the only one left believing in market economy. In a fateful move by the Nobel committee to balance Swedish socialist economist Gunnar Myrdal, Hayek was awarded the 1974 Nobel Prize in Economic Sciences. By that time, he was so obscure that many economists had not even heard of him when the award was announced.

Although many people knew about the problems, one of the first nations to make the turn was none other than the Great Britain. After a long debate led by Keith Joseph, Margaret Thatcher entered Number 10 Downing Street with the mandate to turn the tide. Her single-minded drive took Britain through the hardship of slaying the inflation dragon. By the time of her reelection in 1983, inflation (Retained Price Index) had reduced from 21% in 1980 to 3.7%, but the unemployment rate had just peaked at 11%. Falkland War saved Thatcher. In her second term, she went after the powerful and militant coal miners' union. The miners thought that they could break Thatcher just as they had destroyed Ted Heath's Tory government a decade earlier. They underestimated Thatcher's single-mindedness, her determination, and her absolute hatred of government control. The strike lasted a whole year from 1984 to 1985, before the union crumbled right in front of everybody's eyes.

A year and half after Thatcher started her reforms, a Roosevelt Democrat, Ronald Reagan, entered the White House with the mandate to give the government back to the people. Reagan took the same path as his struggling British soul mate. He gave Paul Volcker unwavering support to slay the inflation dragon and vigorously reduced government interference to economic activities. Against the opposition of his entire cabinet, he successfully passed his tax cut. For a politician, that was hazardous undertaking, but Reagan did not care. It was lucky for Reagan that the American economy was well on its way of recovery when he had to face the voters again in 1984.

Deng Xiaoping started his economic reforms before Thatcher, with his "socialism in the Chinese style" policy. In a spin-free world, it should be called "capitalism under one party dictatorship". The word "socialism" was used to soothe the nerve of the Party conservatives. His complete rebellion to Marxism was best expressed in his motto, "No matter white or black, the cat that catches mice is a good cat." His piecemeal reforms were not nearly as successful as those of Thatcher and Reagan. In fact, if Deng Xiaoping had allowed Zhao Ziyang to carry out Zhao's political reforms, instead of shutting down free elections after 1981 (a series of exciting events that the West had largely ignored), the Chinese commanding heights[5] might have been privatized long ago.

Among the nations that have launched economic reforms, Poland stands out as an example of success. The difficulties with the Polish case were that the Solidarity was originally a labor union. After taking over power, it launched the shock therapy immediately by cutting the government spending and implementing market mechanism at the same time. Solidarity's core members, the blue-collar laborers, were hurt the most, but the leadership stuck to its guns until the market mechanism started to turn the prices around. It was almost an unthinkable feast, but Solidarity captured the moment, and used the opportunity to its maximum potential by making the boldest moves.

Poland did all that with Gorbachev watching closely. To his credit, Gorbachev did not roll tanks into Warsaw, but he failed to apply the Polish model to the Soviet economy when he had the chance. In fact, he was completely inept in reforming the Soviet economy. His hesitation invited the military coup and the Boris Yeltsin revolt, which ended the Soviet Union. Sadly, Yeltsin was no economic white knight either. His actions, in the newly established democratic system, were driven by the political considerations—the need for massive political

---

5.   Lenin used the term to denote industries that were critical to economy (e.g. steel, coal, and railroad industries).

donations so he could defeat his political opponents. Yeltsin created a situation in Russia that voters had no good alternatives in voting booths. If they abandoned him, they had to vote for either the communist conservatives or weak figures like Gorbachev who commanded only a few percent of the votes in presidential elections. Yeltsin's haphazard reforms put the Russian people through so much unnecessary hardship that it was absolutely amazing that they kept on voting for him again and again.

Even North Korea, against Beijing's wish, wanted to establish a free trade zone in Sinuiju. Beijing quickly arrested Yang Bin, a Chinese-born Dutch citizen, who was appointed the chief executive of the zone, which, according to reports, forced Kim Jong Il to consider former Fullerton, California, mayor before giving up the idea for lack of support from Hu Jintao.

The world is certainly a different place now, except in sporadic areas, such as the educational system and the nation's docks, where one can still see the remnants of the government control of yesteryear.

Conspicuously lost in this move toward free market is Japan. After WWII, the Japanese economy took off partly fueled by the powerful export growth. Its success was exemplified by Sony, which took American ideas (e.g., tape recorder), refined them (e.g., walkman), produced products with superior quality and lower costs, and sold them successfully throughout the world. A constant reminder of the Japanese success is on display on the streets and in the parking lots of most U.S. cities. Once when I went to a shopping center in Los Angeles, a friend joked, "Welcome to the Toyota car show." After counting, we found that more than 50% of the cars parked in the lot were Toyotas.

For more than a decade, the Japanese economy was squeezed by the cheap exports from its Asian neighbors and the revived creativity of the U.S. businesses. The Japanese government recognized the problem early on, but fatefully made the wrong move. Instead of taking down the oligarchic rule of *keiretsu* companies and empowering the creativities of the Japanese people, especially the small companies, the Japanese government asserted itself in the development of new technologies and displayed the classic problem of the government operation. (1) It picked wrong technologies; and (2) it stayed with the wrong technologies for too long. For instance, one technology that the Tokyo technocrats picked was the analog high-definition television technology. The idea of analog HDTV could not take off in the U.S. because investors failed to see how the technology could be profitable. Tokyo technocrats did not worry about the financial details and deployed the analog HDTV system in Japan at great cost to the Japanese taxpayers.

When digital technologies began to mature, the American investors quickly realized the potential for the technologies and invested in digital HDTV, which rendered the Japanese analog system—yet to turn any profit—obsolete overnight.

Government bureaucrats tend to pick the wrong ideas because of their propensity toward ostentatiousness. Profitability is not their primary concern, if at all. Once they pick the project, their reputation and pride are on the line. It is next to impossible for them to stop an ongoing project for reasons such as grim profitability outlooks. After all, they are not burning their own money. Another example to demonstrate the Japanese government's bad decision-making power was the Seikan Tunnel that links Honshu and Hokkaido. Digging commenced in 1964 and the commercial service did not start until March 1988 when air travel was quicker and almost just as cheap.

Some argued that the Japanese government had directed its automakers to take advantage of the oil crisis by making small cars while the American automakers were making gas-guzzlers. That argument ignored the fact that the Japanese automakers had *always* made small cars in Japan *before* the oil crisis. The Japanese government simply came afore to take the credit that it did not earn.

Government involvement and the *keiretsu* rigidity have made the Japanese internal economy highly stale. In Japan, the best Japanese minds go to large companies and become "salary-men", a made-in-Japan term that vividly illustrates the mentality of these people. These people expect to be "taken cared of" by the company for their working career. When a salary-man moves from one company to another, he would become a subject of belittlement. Once, when working for Fujifilm, I questioned the validity of some belittling jokes aimed at a particular Japanese marketing manager. The reply I got was, "He is from Hitachi."

The problem is not with the Japanese people, but the Japanese system. For instance, many Japanese colleagues of mine expressed admiration to me that I could, on my own volition, leave China and explore the U.S. Under the salary-men culture, they do not dare to make a move like that.

Some American managers might consider Japan as teamwork heaven, and might love to work there. The problem is that such systems are often stale, which is a deadly shortcoming in today's rapidly changing world.

In addition, Japan is currently experiencing the problem that will start to haunt the U.S. in a few decades—the graying of the population. There is a paramount need for the Japanese economy to become more efficient in order for fewer people to serve more without reducing overall living standard, but the Japanese government and industrial oligarchs are refusing any reforms because they are too comfortable.

The Japanese economy desperately needs a shock therapy to liberate currently suppressed smaller companies and individuals. The key is that the Japanese government must break up the *keiretsu* and allow its members to fail. The banks that have been rolling over mountains of non-serviceable debts are the best candidates to lead the parade.

Facing reticent politicians, the Japanese people made a move. Against the party elders for the first time, they elected Junichiro Koizumi, but Koizumi's reform measures were too weak to make a difference. The Japanese people have to get bolder, and elect someone more stubborn and less team-spirited than Margaret Thatcher or, for Japan-watchers, Masahisa Naitoh[6] to administer the shock therapy. As long as they fail to do that, the Japanese economy would continue dwindling. After Nikkei (the Japanese equivalent of Dow Jones Industrial Average) hit its high of 38,916 on December 29, 1989, it went for a dive to below 8,000. For a couple of years, it has been hovering between 10,000 and 12,000.

With the high educational level of the Japanese population, the Japanese culture of hard working, and the Japanese ingenuity that I can personally bear witness, there is no doubt that Japan can have a bright future, but the reforms must come first. So far, the Japanese society has been wasting its energy on resisting reforms.

Once upon the time, a certain segment of the American academic elite believed that the future of the world belonged to Japan. Many of them now think that the future belongs to China, which remains to be un-free and un-democratic. These people won't do well in the stock market.

The American new economy is certainly not problem-free. In the so-called jobless recovery of 2002, under historically low interest rate with low inflation, companies terminated technological development projects in midstream not because of government intrusions, but because they were running scared. Their confidence for innovation was lost. In the wake of the technology slump, high-tech experts and development managers were massively laid off, without any foreseeable chance of getting back to do what they were professionally trained to do

---

6.   Masahisa Naitoh was a former official of the Ministry of International Trade and Industry (MITI) who was fired because he campaigned for deregulation.

with years of experiences. Unable to find anything to do, technology experts stayed on the sideline collecting unemployment benefit, and then switched to other fields, such as real-estate brokerage.

Hewlett Packard put out a theme ad in 2002 that it was building 24-hour government in China. Reading that ad, I thought little about HP, but just hoped that it was not an indication that the United States no longer provided the environment for technological innovation, forcing the U.S. companies to be innovative elsewhere.

Regardless of the problems, the sea changes of the economic system prove the point that changes are possible. It must be fascinating for people like Hayek to see the world's collective subconscious filters change twice in their lifetime. In Hayek's case, it must have been especially sweet because the second turn was in his direction. Different nations have their different stories of making the turn. All of them are spectacular. This is what heroic ages are made of—heroes coming from nowhere to point out the wrongs of the collective subconscious filters, make people see that the emperor has no cloth on, and successfully deploy new ones that few support in the beginning.

The macroscopic-scale change of the economic systems is more difficult, more painful, and more violent than alcoholics quitting booze, because fundamental policy changes cannot be conducted incrementally. Zhao Ziyang tried to reform the Chinese political system by implementing free elections incrementally in 1980. According to his plan, local free elections were held first. After Li Shuxian, the wife of famous dissident Fang Lizhi, was elected as People's Delegates in that election, the Communist Party conservatives put an end to free elections.

The economic systems have to be changed in whole sale fashion, known to economists as shock therapy. Just as alcoholics quitting cold turkey, such sudden changes carry many risks and side effects. Successful handling of ensuing problems requires extremely high skills. Since shock therapy is the only way to bring changes, reformers have to deal with all the problems effectively enough that the oppositions won't be able to use the problems to stop the shock therapy itself. That is difficult because people always blame reformers for their problems that are often not related to the reform at all. The U.S. educational system has successfully resisted any fundamental change for two centuries after Thomas Jefferson elucidated the solution. Zhao Ziyang was put to *de facto* house arrest for 16 years before his death in 2005.

Shock therapies are necessary because opponents should not be given the opportunity to implement countermeasures. Their determination is shown by the bitterness of the air traffic controllers who were fired by Ronald Reagan more than 20 years ago, not to mention the British coal miners.

Still, such changes are necessary. We know now that the American air traffic controllers and the British coal miners did not suffer in vain, because after their pain, the economy took off for a two-decade boom. Some believe that Reagan's firing of the air traffic controllers was his best foreign policy move, as it announced to the world that he meant what he said, and ultimately led to the collapse of the Soviet Union.

The starting point of the change, in a democratic society, is the public consensus that things have to be changed. "I'm as mad as hell and I'm not going to take this anymore"[7] is a good illustration of the sentiment of the people who put Ronald Reagan into the White House to initiate the historic reforms.

Since the voters are not determined to that degree to reform the educational system, we see no fundamental change in that area.

One day, when the public puts up adequate support, reform measures (e.g., the implementation of the voucher system) would burn through the bureaucratic nonsense like wild fire. The effect would be no less phenomenal than the Reagan-Thatcher-Deng economic revolution that has changed the world.

---

7.   *Network,* Warner Studios (1976)

8

The Government

It is often difficult to separate politics from economy, because economic wellbeing ranks above all other political concerns in both democratic and totalitarian systems. In the U.S. , most presidential campaigns are waged over economic issues. For instance, both Jimmy Carter and George Bush Sr. lost their second election primarily because of economic problems. Both Ronald Reagan and Bill Clinton won their second term because of preferable economic conditions. When economy is doing badly, people might not understand what is wrong, but they can, and normally do, blame incumbents, and vote for the challengers. The act is known as protest vote; and the phenomenon "It's the economy, stupid." Even in dictatorship systems, where people could not vote, under harsh economic conditions, leaders would face internal challenges. Mao Zedong was pushed aside after his disastrous Giant Leap Forward Movement in 1958. Despite constant efforts by the Chinese authorities to inject favorable images of Mao Zedong into the minds of the Chinese people, the shadow of the economically disastrous Cultural Revolution and the Giant Leap Forward Movement still remains. Deng Xiaoping was a different story. Despite his Tiananmen Square Massacre in 1989, the Chinese people would remember him as the person who successfully launched the economic reforms.

Before discussing government, we need a better understanding of governmental processes. Modern governmental functions could be separated into two categories—informational and non-informational processes. A computer can conduct informational processes, such as tax reporting, welfare, legislation, finance, litigations, international agreements, and government contract management. Computer alone cannot carry out non-informational operations, such as police, jails, military, nuclear weapons programs, and fire departments, although all non-informational operations have heavy informational aspects. Some operations are mixtures of the two. For instance, immigration contains informational part such as visa applications, and non-informational part such as border control.

Election is probably the most important informational processes in democratic politics. Of course, we all want to sit down and discuss issues with candidates before making up our minds. If possible, we want to work with the candidates for a few weeks to see how they handle different situations, but that would never happen. Statistically speaking, nobody discusses issues with national candidates long enough to get a sense of them. The candidate's information is delivered to the voters mono-directionally, through media reports, political advertisements, campaign rallies where the candidates give identical stump speeches, and direct mailing, which is the most costly way for candidates to deliver their messages.

Occasionally, a candidate would run on ideals, such as FDR, Churchill, Thatcher, and Reagan. These candidates may have tactical message delivery problems, but they know what they are campaigning for and don't need others to work out their main themes. For instance, although Atlee took advantage of Churchill by impressing on the British voters that Churchill was kowtowing to the ideas of this foreign fellow Friedrich August von Hayek, everyone knew that the campaign was about whether the government should run the economy. Even if Atlee had not used Hayek's name as a weapon against Churchill, it would be difficult for Churchill to make up the difference (Tables 8.1.), because the hearts of the British people were not with Churchill. Likewise, if Reagan had done worse tactically in 1980, Carter probably would not have won anyway (Tables 8.2.).

Table 8.1. 1945 British election.

	Labor	Tory	Other
Popular vote	48.9%	37.2%	14.0%
Parliament Seats	393 (63%)	197 (32%)	33 (5%)

Table 8.2. 1980 U.S. Presidential Election Results

	Reagan	Carter	Anderson
Popular vote	51.4%	41.6%	7.0%
Electoral	489	49	0

For others, who do not have strong ideals, campaign strategies and tactics become more important. Nixon ran as market conservative, but after he entered the White House, he realized that the best way to get support was by implementing more government control rather than less. As a result, he won his second term with a landslide. In 1992, Clinton defeated Bush with a simple "change" theme, which precisely caught Bush's weakness. He won the 1996 presidential campaign with his "triangulation" strategy, devised by Dick Morris—a Republican consultant. Under the strategy, Clinton worked with the Republican Congress to pass republican legislations, which pulled out the rug under Bob Dole, his Republican opponent.

In a sense, political strategists, image experts, pollsters, and managers have one job: to manufacture positive images of their candidates and negative images of the opponents. The whole point of campaigns is for the candidates to stick their messages in the minds of the voters while making them ignore the opponents' messages. When Michael Dukakis rode in a tank to display his military aptitude but looked like a fool, the Bush (Sr.) campaign put that image on Bush's political ads and played it repeatedly to make the point that Dukakis was no military leader. In that round of competition, Bush's message, instead of Dukakis', stuck in the minds of the voters.

"The key to running a campaign on the cheap," according to Dick Morris, "is to avoid spending money on anything other than projecting a message. Rich candidates squander millions on headquarters, staff, duplicative consultants and the like. A candidate needs enough money to get his or her message across."[1] The key to any campaign is that message. If the candidate does not have one, political consultants must help him build it. When Clinton was frustrated by the 1994 midterm election, Morris helped Clinton destroy Newt Gingrich first, so Republicans had to put up Bob Dole against him in 1996. Then, Clinton applied his "triangulation" strategy to annihilate Dole.

To create the best campaign messages, campaign consultants use the modern marketing theories—the same ones used by companies to sell cars and shampoo. One of the most effective tools is market segmentation, which cuts the population into many homogeneous segments and studies the behaviors of each segment individually. With the understanding of each segment, before releasing a message, consultants could assess the impact of the messages over each segment and therefore the entire population. Karl Rove, the campaign architect of Bush Jr. , is an expert on segmentation.

---

1.   Dick Morris: *The New Prince: Machiavelli Updated for the Twenty-First Century,* Renaissance Books, 1999

Of course, even with the help of marketing tools, the production of the messages is still creative work. Clinton was a master strategist himself. In 1992, his "change" theme worked out splendidly because he decisively won one segment of voters—the so-called soccer moms. In 1996, his "triangulation" strategy left Dole with no chance whatsoever.

Professionalized elections become scary as campaign consultants perfect the fine art of manufacturing effective political messages and making them stick in the minds of voters, possibly shielding the true faces of the candidates from the public. Ed Rollins, who ran Ross Perot's 1992 campaign for a while before clashes with the candidate forced him out of the Perot campaign, had complained that Perot was no presidential timber, but riding on the high tide of public resentment against Bush (Sr.) and the worry that a Democrat might turn back the Reagan Revolution. According to Rollins, Perot could have won a well-managed campaign.[2] When wrong people are elected to Congress, the damage is limited because it takes the majority to make a decision. Even if 10% of the members are mistakes, Congress may still discharge its responsibilities reasonably. For the office of the president, such mistakes could be costly.

With the messages set, candidates need money to deliver them to the public. Incumbents have a significant advantage, because they have been collecting money throughout their stay in office from more sources than their challengers. They also have closer relations with top political consultants.

Such a system favors Washington insiders. Many people who have done grassroots political work are frustrated because they run into brick walls when their issues reach Washington. In Washington, money, skill, and most of all, years of connections are required to get anything done. The system disfavors amateurs. People with reason but not money, when running against powerful vested interests, have little chance of winning. With weakened grassroots, the importance of the consultants and lobbyists is further enhanced. Many successful political careers have been launched inside the Capital Beltway. For instance, George Mitchell, who was the senate majority leader and went on to be the chairman of the Walt Disney Company, started his political career as executive assistant to Senator Edmund Muskie inside the capital beltway.

Facing the reality of political campaigns, many qualified candidates refuse to run for offices, resulting in the decrease of the quality of political candidates. Often, voters are offered two bad choices. In the 2002 California governor race,

---

2.   Ed Rollins: *Bare Knuckles and Back Rooms*, Broadway (1996)

neither Gray Davis nor Bill Simon was qualified for the job. In a way, Davis won by using Clinton's 1996 playbook. He got rid of a more competitive Republican candidate—former Los Angeles mayor Richard Riordan—by running negative campaign ads against Riordan before the Republican primary. With the support of the White House, Bill Simon was duly elected the Republican candidate and was duly defeated by Davis. Davis was subsequently impeached by popular vote and replaced by Arnold Schwarzenegger.

After the application of Marxism-Keynesianism, government today is an information monstrosity even after the Reagan Revolution. For instance, the environmental laws that define the allowed amount of release of every single chemical in every fashion into the environment are so complex that even the experts have trouble from time to time to judge whether a release is legal.

For most Americans, tax codes are the most complex and nagging laws that they have to deal with. Although many people use accountants to help them fill out tax forms, they still have to do the preparation work. There are many politicians in Washington pushing for the idea of a flat tax rate, under the banner of process simplification. That, of course, is a political sleight of hand, because today's information technologies could handle the progressive tax calculation just as easy as flat tax rate. The complication comes from the unclear tax codes that allow different ways to treat income or expense items.

Even with current tax rates, IRS[3] could still use the latest information technologies to relieve most of the tax-reporting headaches of average taxpayers. Today, IRS has all the information about wages (W-2 and 1099), interests, dividends, realized investment incomes, mortgage interest payments, etc. For charitable donations, the government could require the receiving party to file a report, so there is no need for the taxpayers to be bothered with the reporting of their deductible donations. For most people, IRS only needs to ask the taxpayers whether they have changed their status in the past year (e.g., married or had a child), received additional taxable income, or incurred unreported deductible expenses (e.g., moving expenses). The tax reporting process for most of the people could be as easy as logging on to the IRS website, putting in their social security number and password, and clicking on "no status change", "no additional taxable income" and "no additional deductible expense" buttons. Refunds would be in their bank account within 24 hours.

---

3.   The United States Internal Revenue Services

When I talked to some IRS people in El Segundo, California, in 1997, they were quite interested in the ideas, but pointed out that lawmakers in Washington had to make the first move. Today, the majority (64% in 2001[4]) of the Americans has Internet access at home. For others, Internet access is a short trip away to their local libraries. The government resistance to the implementation of information technologies is entirely political. For instance, tax attorneys and accountants are groups that lobby heavily in Washington. If the federal government allows the application of information technologies in tax reporting, many tax attorneys and accountants would lose their jobs. Politicians could use that leverage to extract political donations for their effort to uphold the status quo.

There are roughly 100 million taxpayers in the U.S. If each of them saves 10 hours with the new system, it translates to the saving of 1,000,000,000 hours for the nation. If each taxpayer saves, on average, $100 on accountants, tax attorneys, software, books, printing, copying, traveling, and other tax reporting related expenses, it is a $10,000,000,000 annual saving. Also, it could save the federal government billions for printing and mailing the tax forms to businesses and taxpayers, sorting the tax reports from businesses and taxpayers, entering data into computer, checking the accuracy of the reports, and auditing businesses and taxpayers[5]. With the consideration of the psychological pain that the information system would alleviate, it is simply amazing that the government manages to resist the implementation of such a system for so long so successfully.

Nasty informational operations are everywhere. For instance, the immigration application process causes many people headaches and keeps many immigration lawyers in business. Once again, it does not use available information technologies. Since these government agencies do not have customers in mind, they make their customers fit their behaviors. When a green card holder tries to apply for citizenship, he has to figure out what forms that USCIS requires him to fill, find these forms, fill them out, and mail them. Even when USCIS automates some of the processes, it asks applicants to fill out the forms online. Today, many people could not even figure out what forms they should fill, and have to hire lawyers to help them do the work.

4.　http://cyberatlas.internet.com/big_picture/geographics/article/
　　0,5911_919221,00.html (1/6/2003)
5.　Today, IRS spends $10 billion a year to collect taxes. The same information system would also help states reduce their expenditures on tax collection.

No private companies work this way. When a customer buys books from Amazon.com, for example, she only needs to type the book title or the author's name and hit "search" button, and views everything that fits the description. After she decides what to buy, the website would ask the necessary questions, such as credit card information, to complete the transaction. USCIS could do the same on its website. First, the applicant finds the task, for instance "seeking citizenship by a green card holder". Second, after the website finds out who that person is, it would only ask for the information that USCIS does not already have. After receiving the necessary information, the website would tell the applicant immediately whether the application is provisionally approved according to the received information and policy. In the case that the application is provisionally approved, the website asks the applicants to mail necessary documentations to complete the approval process.

One person's saving is another's loss of income. In the IRS case, accountants, tax lawyers and government paper pushers stand to lose; in the USCIS case, immigration lawyers and government paper pushers are on the losing end. The problem is that those who resist change are much more effective than those who would benefit from the change. In the end, the taxation system benefits accountants and government workers rather than taxpayers; the immigration process serves the interests of immigration lawyers and government workers rather than the policy; and the educational system benefits teachers and government bureaucrats rather than students.

Once again, the nature's law is against us. The problem here is that when a minority has managed to take advantage of the majority, the minority would put up some of their earnings to form a protective mechanism to keep taking advantage of the majority. On the minority side, lawyers, accountants, and government workers use already collected money to carry out determined fights, because automation means that they would lose much, if not all, of their income. On the majority side, it is difficult to organize a coherent and determined political fight since (1) the loss is small for each member, (2) the loss is invisible (e.g., IRS spends approximately $100 per taxpayer to collect taxes), and (3) the majority has to put up fresh money to launch a reform movement in Washington.

Another difficulty for the implementation of information technologies is the convoluted relations between the government and its existing IT[6] contractors. In many cases, when the government department issues a request for bid, it often

---

6.   Information Technologies

has the winner in mind. It is useless for anyone else to bid on the government projects if they are not already on the inside track. In order to penetrate the system, many companies have to hire insiders—responsible people who have retired from the targeted government departments. Simply responding to those requests is a waste of time. When I attempted to do business with government, the general contractor who had the government in its pocket squashed me. At least in my experience, government contract is full of game playing so one could not just focus on doing the business.

To make people feel better about the government, it undertakes many deceitful maneuvers. One of the biggest spins is the so-called social security trust fund. Today, the government levies 13% of personal income from the employers and employees into the fund. First, it is not a fund. People certainly pay 13% of the income into the fund account, but it would be taken out by the already entitled retirees. In fact, entitled retirees withdraw from the fund so quickly that the fund is running out of money with increasingly unrealized obligations. In other words, social security has become an out-and-out entitlement program. Second, when the general treasury needs money, it "borrows" from the trust fund. As long as the U.S. treasury remains in debt, it has no money to pay back the trust fund. When the trust fund runs out of money, the treasury has to borrow money from the open market to pay the social security obligations, making social security exactly an entitlement program from financing perspective. Third, politicians do not distinguish the two. When Clinton reported that the government was out of deficit spending, he meant the combined incomes and outlays (i.e. general taxation income and social security income minus general expenditure and social security outlays). In every sense, social security tax is part of the general treasury and the social security payment is an entitlement program. The government should simplify the process by integrating the 13% social security tax into the general taxation.

Government spinning ran the full circle when a government employee advanced an argument to me that the government was so inept that it would screw up the implementation of information technologies, and thus should not be entrusted to undertake the task.

One of the informational functions of the government is to fund scientific research. As in all cases that the government hands out money, there is a competition for it. Unfortunately, it is a gaming process. For instance, through distributing funds, the government essentially decides whether the society should first cure AIDS or Parkinson's disease. To play the game, all diseases need to have their lobbying organizations in Washington to assure that they get the appropriate funding. AIDS representatives have done an outstanding job in this regard. To any sane people, it is absurd to imagine that every disease needs its expensive operation in Washington to lobby against other diseases with political connections and campaign contributions for government research funds.

When working in Washington as a lobbyist, I was told the set strategy numerous times by numerous people. If an organization wants to forward a cause, it needs to find two senators and two House members from each party who are devoted to its cause. Then, it can work on other members to get support. For any legislation to pass, it needs to budget for at least five years (i.e., a lot of money). Even after the legislation has passed, it should keep its presence in Washington to make sure that Congress won't undo the law.

Under that mechanism, government often launches noble tasks to devastating results. One of the primary examples is the notorious public housing projects. A more recent example is the Telecommunications Act of 1996, which skewed the market by putting the giants at a pricing disadvantage in favor of smaller companies. The distortions caused irrational activities of the players in the market, gave many Wall Street crooks opportunities to take advantage of the law, and ultimately collapsed many telecommunication firms.

Information technologies could make non-informational processes more efficient and more transparent, but could not replace them, because one could not stop crime with information alone. Still, non-informational processes are full of informational elements. Rudy Giuliani reduced crimes in New York by using the real-time crime information system to direct police patrols.

One of the major obstacles for the implementation of the information technologies is that the people in the government are used to leveraging information access as part of their power plays. Those people who are "in" would get information; and those "out" won't. Prior to 9/11 terrorist attack, FBI stopped giving terrorist related information to John O'Neill, its top anti-terrorist expert, because the FBI brass, i.e., Louis Freeh (FBI Director 1993–2001) and his cronies, did not think that O'Neill was playing their games. Despite that O'Neill devoted his life to FBI, he lived as an outsider and was finally squeezed out. Who cares? Nobody is irreplaceable. Someone would continue his work. One may say that FBI facilitated the 9/11 attack by squeezing out O'Neill.[7]

---

7.   Murray Weiss: *The Man Who Warned America: The Life and Death of John O'Neill, the FBI's Embattled Counterterror Warrior,* Regan Books (2003)

The contrary example is Robert Hanson, who spent much of his time hanging around Freeh, Freeh's church, and Freeh's family, playing the bureaucratic game, and carrying on a successful FBI career before he was caught as a spy.

There are many other cases that the bureaucracy inside FBI hurt the interests of the U.S. Since its beginning, FBI's counter-espionage operation has been a crapshoot. In the nuclear weapon programs, Leo Szilard (1898–1964) and Robert Oppenheimer (1904–1967)—two of the most outstanding nuclear scientists who contributed enormously to the Manhattan Project—had problems with FBI.

FBI's latest display of counter-espionage ineptitude was its case against Wen-Ho Lee (1939–). With détente, American weapon scientists started to meet their Soviet, and later Chinese, counterparts. Precious information about the Russian and Chinese weapon programs was obtained through those interactions; and mutual understanding reduced the risk of an accidental nuclear war. Such interactions were also a game. The key was not to give out information that you did not intend to give out but get information that the other side did not mean to provide. All sides made conscious decisions on who were allowed to play the game. The authorities of Los Alamos National Lab allowed Lee to play this game with Chinese scientists. Then, with evidence that the secret of making compact H-Bomb was lost to China, FBI needed a scapegoat. Conveniently, Lee became its dedicated spy without any convincing evidence, let alone evidence to prove the case beyond reasonable doubt which was required to convict him in criminal court. By leaking the story to media, FBI deflected the public attention but made Lee the embodiment of evil. The irony was that it also leaked the technical details of the H-Bomb to the media to make its argument. Now, not only the Chinese, but also everyone else in the world, know how to build compact H-Bombs.

The lab summarily fired Wen-Ho Lee, who was the first ever LANL employee to be fired. Ultimately, in court settlement, he admitted one count of felony misconduct of downloading classified data in violation of the lab Rules, which were frequently violated by not only the researchers but also people in the intelligent community.

Lee's case caused a wave of terror in Los Alamos, as well as other national labs. If Lee, who had spent most of his career as a researcher at Los Alamos (since 1974), was permitted to interact with the Chinese weapon experts, and had done undercover work for FBI, could be so nonchalantly destroyed by FBI, FBI could do that to anyone. FBI created sheer terror in the national labs that only Joseph McCarthy had caused before.

With the proper implementation of information technologies, John O'Neill should have automatic access to all terrorist information. Such access could only be terminated with official demotion. With case evidence available to more people, we have a better chance for someone to stand up and say that the emperor had no cloth on, i.e., there is no case against Leo Szilard, Robert Oppenheimer, or Wen-Ho Lee. With transparency, bureaucratic game players like Robert Hanson would have less chance to be promoted.

Today's situation is that, without explicit support from the president, people who dare to speak out, such as William von Raab and David Kessler, do not last long in the government, while those who play the game for their personal gain remain forever. Incidentally, John O'Neill was nowhere near speaking out against FBI when he was squeezed out of the Bureau. As fate goes, on September 11, 2001, as security chief of the World Trade Center, O'Neill was killed by the terrorists, underlining the fact that his personal struggle against the terrorists was lost.

The bureaucratic problem was so severe for Deng Xiaoping that, when he started the economic reforms in China, he had to get rid of essentially everyone in the government by implementing the absolute rule (i.e., no exception is allowed) that everyone above 65 was to retire immediately and those above 58 were to receive no promotion. That policy weakened the resistance to his reforms. Unbeknownst to Deng, the side effect was that the newly promoted young officials corrupted quickly. Seeing they held unchecked power, businesses quickly learned that they had to play the game and take care of these officials. When Deng Xiaoping was still around, there was still fear. After Jiang Zemin took over, the corruption became open and notorious.

Westerners might not appreciate Deng Xiaoping enough for what he accomplished in China. Without mandate from the people, Deng had to rely on his ability to reach consensus at top and dictatorship iron fist to deal with everybody else. Till death, he did not understand the tragedy he had played under this wicked system.

Despite offering of lip services, the Party conservatives never supported Deng Xiaoping's reform measures. When Deng proposed to open up Shanghai for economic reforms in early 1980s, the Party conservatives stopped him, forcing him to open up Shenzhen, a fishing village bordering Hong Kong, putting off the reforms of Shanghai for more than a decade. Before he died, Deng Xiaoping cursed those leftist conservatives that if he had been allowed to reform Shanghai, the entire China would look different. (Unlike in the U.S. , "conservatives" in

China denotes leftists who want the government to control the lives of the people. The word is used as an antonym to "reformers", who want to change all that and are known to the Chinese as the rightists.)

An example of Deng Xiaoping's toughness is his interaction with Margaret Thatcher. Thatcher, not a softy by any means, went to see Deng in 1982 to discuss the future of Hong Kong. She thought that she could return the sovereignty to China but retain British management. Deng reportedly yelled at her with profanities about the dirty deeds that Britain had forced on the Chinese people throughout the history and told her that they ended with him. Thatcher was so shocked that when she walked out of the Great Hall of the People, the iron lady stumbled down the steps.

The tragedy of Deng Xiaoping is that when Thatcher wanted to resist the effort of European integration among other things, the British people could stop her; but when Deng Xiaoping resisted political reforms, the Chinese people could not stop him from ordering tanks into Tiananmen Square. In the end, Thatcher is remembered as the person who turned the world toward market economy; but Deng Xiaoping, in the minds of many in the world, the butcher of Tiananmen Square.

Ronald Reagan displayed his leadership traits, as he spoke out for the unpopular issues such as abortion. In U.S. -Soviet relations, he boldly switched from the policies of détente to that of confrontation by speaking out against the evils of communism.

Reagan was confronted with considerable obstacles. His delegating management style might have allowed him to survive eight trying years in Washington, but his revolution burned out all his major lieutenants. Mike Deaver, who was close to Reagan for some 30 years, had to quit completely because stress had finally restarted his alcoholic problems. Ed Meese retreated to the Department of Justice; and Jim Baker to Treasury. When the inept Don Regan moved into the White House, disasters loomed soon.

Heroes enter their offices to make changes. With all admitted shortcomings (e.g., Tiananmen Square for Deng Xiaoping, and Iran-Contra for Ronald Reagan), they go against nature's antagonistic laws (e.g., Prisoner's Dilemma) and our bodies' faulty design (e.g., subconscious filters). They, the revolutionary practitioners rather than theorists, lead the human society by implementing ideas. After the Reagan Revolution, the U.S. needs another batch of heroes in the government to unleash the power of American ingenuity. Just like in the Reagan

Revolution, there is no guarantee that the reformers are going to prevail over reactionaries such as the teachers associations. The only certainty is that they are going to burn out a lot of people.

Government is more problematic than other systems because of its monopoly. The educational system, which has to be neither under the government nor monopolistic, displays the strong reactionary energy against any changes, and has successfully rejected every substantial change so far. Reagan's philosophy is quite simple: Since it is not possible to inject competition in the core functions of government, let's reduce the power of the government as much as possible, and allow the private sector to take over.

The best kind of government is no government. According to Lao Zi, people under the optimum government live in peace and know the existence of neither their neighbors nor government. In today's democratic society, that is impossible, because if the majority ignores the government, the minority that actively tries to influence the government would take advantage of the majority, just like the educational system.

In administration, government faces several problems, besides bureaucratic problems that are of the same nature as big businesses, only to a greater extent because government is the biggest employer around with monopoly. Compared to other countries, American government is reasonably successful in self-controlling its monopolistic power, especially after Ronald Reagan. The governmental power in many other countries is outright abusive. In China, for instance, nobody could get anything done without bribing a chain of government officials. The process and cost have been built into the normal business practices that few business people think much about it.

In the United States, besides bureaucratic slowness, the problems are of a much lesser degree and sporadic. Most of them are concentrated in areas where a determined minority could deceit the public with its superior funding and swindling skills. The Game Theory basis of this problem is that it is much more difficult for the taxpayers in general to get together and fix problems such as education, than for the minority to put together a lot of money and use class-struggle theories to fight against any politicians who dare to suggest reform. The result is that the majority loses in a democracy. When a minority could overwhelm the majority at an issue as visible and sexy as education, one could easily imagine how much a determined minority could do to a less visible and less sexy issue.

Luckily, much of the government work is information processing. Today's information technologies could solve most of the problems in the informational processes. The key is, once again, the fight between the government bureaucrats and the people. For companies using information technologies, such as Amazon.com, they make their systems understandable. Government is different. Even when they are legally required to release certain information, they would make the information so convoluted that it does not make sense. Under the "No Child Left Behind" law, standard tests are implemented, but the published test results are confusing to say the least. The 2004 STAR[8] result indicates that 0% of the 9th grader at Arcadia High School[9] are considered advanced under "CST General Mathematics (Grades 6 & 7 Standards)". That sounds pretty bad to me. Reasonable people would interpret that no 9th graders could be considered advanced under the 6th and 7th grade standard. But under "CAT/6 Mathematics", 65% of the 9th graders scored "Above 75th NPR[10]". According to STAR website, this means that 65% of the 9th graders at Arcadia High scored as well as or better than 75% of the students nationwide. If we were to trust the test results, Arcadia High's 9th graders are actually quite good compared to their peers in the nation, as 65% of them are above the 75% percentile, but on an absolute level, when measured by the "Grades 6 & 7 Standards", none of those 65% could be considered "advanced". The conclusion sounds like an indictment of the math level of the students nationwide. Arcadia High is within walking distance from my home. I personally know as a matter of fact that, under any reasonable standard for 6th and 7th graders, some of the 9th graders have to be considered advanced. The best of the Arcadia High's 9th graders are not only advanced using any reasonable standard for 6th and 7th graders, but are advanced using any reasonable standard for 9th, 10th, or even 11th graders. The best at Arcadia High are the best in the nation.

Under political pressure, the educational system yielded by allowing standard testing, but it annulled much of the effect with inadequate reporting. Parents should not be required to understand CST or CAT/6. They should be told the result without bureaucratic mumbo jumbo. Most parents want to know how well their children are doing in their schools and how well their schools are doing compared to other schools. They also want to know the historical scores of stu-

---

8.   Standard Testing And Reporting. See http://star.cde.ca.gov/star2004/viewreport.asp (7/18/2005)

9.   Under Los Angeles County and Arcadia Unified School District

10. National Percentile Rank

dents who have made it to Harvard, UC Berkeley[11], UCLA[12], CSU LA[13], and PCC[14].

The solution is simple. For instance, a virtual town hall could be established over the Internet to discuss and identify particular pieces of information. And the government could legislate to compel STAR to release such information.

The political fight to implement these changes, however, would be anything but simple. The vested interests would resist change every step of the way, starting with the establishment of an Internet town hall. Even if the government is required by law to set up an Internet town hall, it would hire its cronies to put up something that few could understand.

Here, nature's antagonistic laws such as Prisoner's Dilemma prevent the government from doing the right things. The only way toward victory is for the president to be personally involved in the development of the technologies with competent people, because game players would ruin the projects by squandering funds and claiming victories when their projects have completely failed.

If the concealment and manipulation of information in the executive and legislative branches of government are only incidental to the government operations, misinformation, misleading, and manipulation of information are of the very essence of the legal proceedings, which is the third pillar of our democracy.

Whenever a dispute reaches trial, whether it is people versus people (i.e., civil litigation), or government (which often calls itself "the People") versus people (i.e., criminal prosecution), it is an adversarial and argumentative process that the most important step is for parties to make juries (in the case of jury trials) or judges (in the case of bench trials) to believe their version of the facts. The "fact finding" step is most important because parties (i.e., plaintiffs' lawyers through their choice of causes of action; and defenses' lawyers through their choice of defenses) and the judges (who interpret applicable laws) choose and determine the law. With favorable facts, it is easy to convince juries to apply judge's instructions regarding applicable laws and reach verdicts in their favor.

In other words, manipulation of information (a.k.a. facts) is primarily what lawyers do. In law schools, there is a saying: "Who care about laws? That's paralegal's work." In Bar Examinations, if an examinee forgets the applicable law, he

---

11. University of California at Berkeley
12. University of California at Los Angeles
13. California State University, Los Angeles
14. Pasadena City College, a community college that is a couple of blocks away from Caltech

could make up the law, apply it to the fact pattern, pass the exam, and be admitted to the Bar (i.e., be certified as a lawyer). The primary job of the lawyers is to make juries see facts their way. In the O. J. Simpson trial, the defense team convinced the jury that racial hatred of the investigators tainted the evidence to the point that it did not constitute evidence "beyond reasonable doubt". In the Michael Jackson trial, defense team convinced the jury that Jackson did not commit any crime, because his acts of allowing children to sleep in his bedroom did not reach the level of criminal liability, albeit those acts were less-than-normal.

With less evidence than what the Simpson prosecution team had presented, murder defendants are routinely convicted and sentenced to long jail terms, which means that Simpson's defense team performed abnormally well. In the lawyer circle, that is how one makes more money than the other—by being better manipulators.

If you ask a good attorney the truth in his case, he probably would tell you truth is whatever he could make in court. If you ask a lawyer whether he believes his client, he probably would laugh and say that is not part of his job, which is about how to "make a case for his client". The job of seeking truth from a neutral standpoint belongs to the jury or the judge. In fact, if a lawyer tries to seek truth from a neutral standpoint, he would be violating ethics rules (e.g., breaching the duty of loyalty).

Sales people say whatever necessary to sell their products. Likewise, lawyers do the same to win cases. The motivation is the same: Superior skills bring bigger paychecks. The difference between sales people and lawyers is that sales people handle normally a simple set of facts (i.e., product specifications) while lawyers handle a complex set of facts (i.e., cases). That might have been the reason that lawyers are more successful in politics than those with sales background. Elitists would say that the masses are blind and stupid so they must be manipulated. They would argue that Margaret Thatcher manipulated the masses with Falkland War, because, without that war, she would be voted out of office and wouldn't be able to continue her reform.

For a lawyer to make money, he has to make sure that the client could pay. That is the reason that bad lawyers focus on his clients' wallet rather than the opponent's. It is a problem with the system. To avoid it, the client has to go by the lawyer's reputation instead of his presentation, because bad lawyers who care less about the reality make more impressive presentations than good ones who are more frank about what they could not do. A friend told me that two types of people made good lawyers—the learners and the liars.

The most a lawyer could personally commit to a case is to take it on a contingency fee basis, which is to say that the lawyer would pay for the expenses of the litigation and won't get a penny if he loses the case. The fact is that except in personal injury cases where lawyers could identify insurance coverage or deep pockets, they do not take cases on contingency basis, because, with insurance companies or deep pockets liable, lawyers know that the pending question is not whether but how much they would be paid.

For clients, the problem with hiring lawyers on contingency fee basis is that lawyers decide how much energy they would invest in a case. Also, their recommendations might be tainted by their considerations rather than that of the clients. For instance, if an attorney has 10 reasonably good cases in his hand (say, each with a 20% chance of winning at trial), he might not care about losing a few and thus drive a hard bargain in each case that is just about too hard for his opponents to accept. If the attorney fails to get a good deal and all 10 cases end up in trial, he has just about 90%[15] chance to win at least one of the cases, which, from the onset, is a great deal for the attorney, but for each individual client, they might not want to push that hard. On the contrary, if the attorney has too many cases to deal with, he might want to settle some without a fight so he could concentrate on the more profitable ones. One thing that attorneys do well is to convince the clients to see things their way.

It is a love-hate relationship we have with our lawyers. When we hire a lawyer, we are probably emotionally involved with the case and want some kind of revenge against the adversaries. We want our lawyers to do the dirty work for us, which means to cause most damages and embarrassment to our opponents.

Of course, competent lawyers are happy to charge clients to do just that. I have witnessed a government employee, who was allegedly mistreated by his boss, asking a lawyer how much damage $20,000 could do to his boss. Any lawyer would immediate calculate his cost. Filing fees, court reporter's fee (for depositions), motion fees, and jury fees would run in the neighborhood of $3,000. Based on the fact that most of the work was done by legal assistant, the attorney said that $20,000 was plenty to give his boss a couple of years of continuous high-quality headache, as he would have to hire a lawyer, respond to personal interrogatories, explain to *his* boss why he had to answer interrogatories and attend depositions directed at the government department and face possible public humiliation. This was a good deal for the attorney. Note that the merit of the

---

15.   89.26% to be exact

case never entered the mind of the attorney or the discussion. In fact, the attorney did not care the least whether his client's case against the boss had any merit, and knew that he was about to become a hired dog to attack someone. It was irrelevant whether that someone was innocent.

To anyone who does not know how to navigate through the court system, "my lawyer will call you" is a serious threat. Of course, the attorneys representing the bosses would be happy to defend them against ruthless employees. They, when deciding whether to take the case, would not concern too much about the merit of the case either.

I have seen attorneys going to trial totally unprepared. After judges made remarks about their lack of discovery effort, they rationalized that they didn't want to reveal their masterful strategy to the other side.

Of course, clients can contribute to the problems. After tough bargaining with an attorney on every penny, the attorney might grudgingly take the case. Clients often complain later that lawyers fail to prepare themselves and clients for the trial. When hearing these complaints, I always tell them, "You get what you have paid for." The worst clients refuse to pay lawyers for their services, forcing lawyers to go to small claims courts. In the Los Angeles Chinese community, clients often disappear on immigration attorneys when they are ordered by the small claims court to pay $150 a month to the attorney. Lawyers have to spread that loss among his paying clients.

Many aliens complain that it is hard for them to find a good immigration lawyer, while immigration lawyers complain that there is no way to practice immigration law without lying, because these people look for answers that are too good to be true. An interesting phenomenon in Los Angeles is that some former asylum applicants open up immigration centers to process asylum papers. Without attorney supervision, they tell rosy stories to convince people to apply for asylum as an easy way to adjust status[16], without telling these potential clients that denial would land them directly in removal[17] proceedings. Because it is hard to adjust status based on employment, many people sign up. One applicant told me that she applied for asylum because USCIS did not charge application fees.

These "firms" send the ill-prepared applicants to USCIS asylum interviews with interpreters but without attorneys. Since the quality of the people in these "firms" is nowhere near that of the asylum officers, their clients are slaughtered in asylum offices.

---

16. It is USCIS lingo for applying for permanent resident status inside the U.S.
17. It is USCIS lingo for deportation.

After failing the interviews, these clients are told to marry U.S. citizens before a certain point in the removal proceeding.

The sad part of the story is that as long as these "firms" dish out rosy stories and charge less than lawyers, they would continue to get clients, forcing attorneys to lower the charges with reduced services to compete.

Of course, there are plenty of incompetent attorneys around. Some of them hang around immigration courts looking for clients. Others could not understand the judge because of their bad English.

The English aptitude of some Chinese attorneys is absolutely horrifying. Once, a Chinese lawyer accompanied a Chinese client to a green card interview because she married an American citizen. The immigration officer told the attorney that either his client had to withdraw the application or he would deny it because the first divorce of the American citizen was done in the Dominican Republic and was not recognized by the federal government. The immigration officer told the attorney that the American citizen had to divorce in California because the addresses of both the American citizen and his first wife were in California. The attorney told the client that the problem was that his divorce decree was not translated into English. The certification done by the American Embassy in the Dominican Republic was no good. One year later, the couple went to the immigration interview with the English translation of the divorce decree. They were offered the same two options, so they withdrew again.

These stories make many people cynical about lawyers. They resolve that problem by calling many lawyers in the phone book to compare price. The result is that lawyers have to talk to more people before getting a client. Since many clients compare price, lawyers have to charge less. The situation is so bad that many lawyers work exclusively on marketing and leave the work to assistants in an assembly line fashion.

Attorneys have plenty of opportunities to be cynical about the clients. For example, after losing a criminal case, the defendant was sentenced to community service. Somehow, losing the case did not convince him that his lawyer was not invincible. He went for a half-day and stopped going. When he was summoned to court, he told his lawyer to get him off the hook because that was "what you are paid to do". The lawyer did not even know what to say. In court, the defendant insisted that he showed up on every occasion, and insisted that he signed the registry. The park service people brought all their registration books. Everyone, including the judge, frantically searched for his name in vain for more than an hour. It was absolutely hard to imagine how this gentleman imagined that he could get off the hook with such contempt of court. He probably had seen too many movies and thought that they got the entire O. J. Simpson defense team working for him. When the judge asked for closing argument, his lawyer simply said, "No, your honor." The district attorney also submitted the case without further comment. There was simply nothing to argue.

Of course, there are many adept attorneys helping clients in all areas of law including immigration. The problem is that any problem in this long chain would spark lies: We have untrained Chinese cowboys masquerading as attorneys, lawyers who do not understand the law or speak adequate English, and clients who want to hear only good news or mistakenly think that they know more than their attorneys. One thing I learned in the U.S. early on was that justice is not handed to anyone on a platter, but everyone has a chance to fight for it.

When cases end, clients would see reality, but for many, it is too late.

9

International Relations

Although playing games is almost diplomats' *raison d'être,* international affairs, especially those critical issues involving leading nations, are always determined by brute force. Darwinism rules at the top level, allowing the fittest to dominate.

A general view of the Western history, from Greek, to Rome, to Great Britain, to the United States, for example, agrees with that point. History also seems to indicate that ideas are more important than size, population, or natural resources. Both Rome and Great Britain ruled many times of its population and land mass with primarily ideas, rather than military power. Dominance by military power alone normally does not last long. Genghis Khan's descendants have proved that point.

Before science and democracy changed the West, the Chinese empire had been the wealthiest nation in the world and the leader in Asia. All challenges to China were in the form of foreign invasions. Nobody challenged China's dominance by establishing another cultural center somewhere else. In other words, nations have challenged China with their excellence but never their maturity. The Chinese maturity level was established in the *chunqiu* (ca. 770 B.C.–476 B.C.) and *zhanguo*[1] (476 B.C.–221 B.C.) periods. During the *chunqiu* period, China was separated into hundreds of small states. Wars between the states continuously and consistently reduced the number of them. As states grew bigger, issues such as communication and transportation began to limit their further growth. After the states were annexed to primarily seven, an equilibrium was established. Although land at the border frequently changed hands, no state could threaten the existence of another. This stable period in the Chinese history is known as the *zhanguo* period, when China became a laboratory for all kinds of ideas. Because kings needed to attract thinkers to help them improve their political systems, nobody persecuted thinkers. When they didn't like certain ideas, thinkers could always go to the next country and offer the idea to another king.

---

1. It is also known in the west as the warring state period.

"Scholars from hundreds of schools"[2] in that period developed the Chinese philosophical structure, which became the basis of the Chinese culture. The stability lasted until Qin, one of the seven states, undertook a serious of political reforms, and gained the ability to run a larger state. When Qin started its unification campaign, weaker nations attempted to unite against the invading Qin, but Qin always had the upper hand diplomatically. It took Qin merely 10 years to accomplish that task.

The microcosm of China during that period displayed Darwinism in its rawest form. Every king strived for meritocracy. But since Qin's takeover, generations of emperors spent their energy on suppressing new thoughts because they regarded them as threats to the stability of their state. They almost uniformly adopted the policy of having an uninformed population[3] while developing an informed elite class to help the emperors rule the nation.

Consequently, after the unification in 221 B.C., the Chinese military power has been declining relative to its neighbors with sporadic exceptions such as the early Tang dynasty (618–907). Twice, the entire China was conquered by foreign invaders—the Yuan[4] (1279–1368) and Qing[5] (1644–1911) dynasty. However, unlike Hannibalic War which might have undermined the Hellenic society, no invasion of China undermined the Chinese culture and philosophy.

Incidentally, Gingis Khan's descendents (the Yuan dynasty) refused to adopt the Chinese culture and were overthrown in less than 100 years, but Nuer Hachi's descendants (the Qing dynasty) lasted almost 300 years by actively adopting the Chinese culture and philosophy. At the end of those periods of foreign rule, the Chinese culture remained intact and the foreign cultures were essentially dissolved.

The power of the Chinese culture that was developed in the *chunqiu* and *zhanguo* periods is so strong that the rise of the Western culture fueled by democracy and science has not changed the minds of generations of intellectuals. Many official scholars thought that this was just another "barbarian[6] invasion" that

---

2.   诸子百家
3.   愚民政策
4.   By descendants of Genghis Khan
5.   By Manchurians
6.   Although the word "barbarian" has a pejorative connotation, it has been used by many history books to denote people less culturally developed. Of course, according to multiculturalism, each culture is just as developed as another. I do not subscribe to that theory and think, for instance, the Soviet forced-labor culture was not as well-developed as the American government-regulated culture during the Cold War.

would go away sooner or later. Even today, many Chinese intellectuals honestly agree with the Chinese Communist Party's propaganda that "Western" democracy is not good for China; and the Chinese-style democracy, which is not democracy at all by Western standard, is the only reasonable choice for China.

Mao Zedong never bothered to understand Western political sciences, but spent significant amount of his time studying Sima Guang's *Intelligence Reflected in History*[7].

At the beginning of the 21st century, when the world has adopted the principles of democracy and individual freedom, the Chinese government still resembles the form of the Qin dynasty (221 B.C.–207 B.C.) more than a modern state, and is still ruled by the thoughts of the *zhanguo* thinkers and the suppressing techniques developed by generations of government thinkers since *zhanguo*.

Many agreed with Mao Zedong when he categorized the U.S. and the Soviet Union as the First World, China with all other poor nations as the Third World, and the rest of the developed countries as Second World. In fact, at the end of the WWII, there was only one super power. The Soviet Union was merely a barbarian challenger to the United States because much of the Soviet weapon system, especially the nuclear weapon systems, including the delivering systems, was developed in the fashion that could only be described as economic suicide. For instance, Stalin, as a policy, made all his real and potential critics "enemies of the people" so he could force them to build military-industrial centers. Educated people in the Soviet Union, even in the 1950s, had a low opinion on communism. When my mother was sent by the Chinese government to study in the Soviet Union, she asked whether her fellow undergraduate students regard Stalin (1879–1953) as highly as the Chinese propaganda machine reported. Her classmates laughed and said that she was politically naïve. Without being able to overtake the United States militarily, the Soviet Union had nowhere else to go but facing total economic collapse.

This kind of situations has been quite common throughout history. All superpowers, such as the Roman Empire and the Chinese Empire, are challenged by foreign "barbarians" at the border. The only difference of the Cold War is that modern missile technologies have made it possible for the barbarian at the door to be on the other side of the globe. Transfers from one cultural center to

---

7.   It is a multivolume chronicle of the Chinese history. The Chinese name is: 资治通鉴.

another, such as from Greece to Rome, or from Britain to the United States, are typically peaceful.

It is not possible for the Soviet Union to win the Cold War, because, on one hand, the Soviet Union could not win based on peaceful economic competition; on the other hand, due to the adoption of MAD[8] strategy by both sides, the Soviet Union could not defeat the United States militarily without getting itself destroyed in the meantime. The Soviet leaders faced several bad options: (1) launching an all out war against the United States which was undoubtedly suicidal, (2) doing nothing, (3) admitting the problems and carrying out economic reforms which required the denouncement of almost every policy since the formation of the Soviet Union.

The Soviet Union, in its predictable bureaucratic wisdom, selected Option Two, under which the Soviet Union became poorer and poorer, while the United States got stronger and stronger. After Reagan turned the American economy around, he stopped the policy of détente and started the confrontational policy to put the Soviet Union onto "the ash heap of history"[9].

One of his critical moves was the so-called Strategic Defense Initiative (a.k.a., Star Wars), which called for the development and deployment of a space-based weapon system to intercept Soviet ICBMs[10]. Since these systems would take years to research, perfect, and deploy, in order to keep the MAD stance, the Soviet Union had to start its own SDI research immediately. The problem was that the Soviet Union did not have the money. Ultimately, SDI triggered the collapse of the Soviet Union.

Like the Roman Empire and the Chinese empire, the United States became a superpower in the world because it held a set of unique ideas, such as freedom of speech, freedom of worship, separation of church and states, separation of power in government, etc. The idea of using forced labor to create super weapons against the United States is no comparison.

In fact, the people of the Soviet Union were the best judges themselves. Whenever they had a chance, they would immigrate to the United States. Few

---

8. Mutual Assured Destruction was the Cold War strategy that each side vowed to launch a full scale nuclear attack when it was attacked by nuclear weapons, which would assure the total destruction of the opponent. Since the other side would do the same, the destruction is mutually assured.
9. Ronald Reagan's speech to the British Parliament at Westminster (June 8, 1982)
10. Intercontinental ballistic missiles

Americans, with the freedom to move to the Soviet Union, took that opportunity.

At the beginning of the Tang dynasty (618 A.D.–907 A.D.), Chang'an[11], the capital city, was full of foreigners. People from all over the region went there to study. Before some foreigners attempted to assassinate Li Shimin, the emperor, they held positions throughout the government. Much of the Japanese culture was imported from China at that time.

Today, many Chinese choose to come to the United States not because life here is easy. In fact, with much faster and persistent economic growth in China, it has been much easier to accomplish something there. They come here because of the American culture. In China, for instance, the political dictatorship and economic freedom have created the total collapse of morality, where many female college students, who are by no means poor, moonlight prostitution, and do not feel that there is anything wrong with it. The curricula of elementary, middle, and high schools are so tough that little kids have to work to midnight to finish their homework. Many new immigrants told me that they chose to come to a tougher situation so their kids could have a better life.

In this sense, one may say that the United States has been taking advantage of other nations. For instance, my alma mater, Qinghua University in Beijing, which is consistently ranked number one university in China, has been labeled by many as the preparatory university for American graduate schools. Many gatherings of the Chinese throughout the United States are full of Qinghua graduates. Year after year, the United States gets the best from Qinghua University.

It is quite natural that the friction between the leader and other nations creates animosity. In China, for instance, college students are extremely anti-America. When the United States mistakenly bombed the Chinese embassy in Belgrade, Yugoslavia, on May 7, 1999, the Chinese students led the charge to siege the American Embassy in Beijing. But, when they graduate, they would line up in the Consular Office of the American Embassy to apply for visas to come to the United States. After the 1989 Tiananmen Massacre, I lobbied the U.S. Congress to grant permanent resident status to all Chinese nationals. One of the first objections came from students of Beijing University. They claimed that they risked their lives in the streets of Beijing, but we, in the safety of the United States, wanted to use their effort to gain our green cards.

---

11.   Chang'an was located near today's Xi'an.

Such love-hate relation with the United States also exists in Russia, France, the Middle East, etc. After all, why should anyone be the second class citizen and live in the shadows of the United States? I have heard people saying that Deng Xiaoping launched the economic reform so he did not have to submit to the American leadership. That opinion, of course, is wrong because Deng Xiaoping had said many times that he launched the reform to improve the living standard of the Chinese people.

The Middle Eastern terrorists want to use an easier way to exit the shadows of the United States, thinking that Americans could be scared off their throne.

In other words, the love-hate relationship between China and the U.S. is benign, while the love-hate relationship between the U.S. and the Middle East terrorists is malignant. Of course, under the dictatorship rule of the Chinese Communist Party, China is always one politburo meeting away from switching to a malignant posture, despite that Deng Xiaoping has made it clear to the Chinese leaders that, for 50 years, China should not challenge the United States in international affairs[12]. Although there are signs recently, such as the much publicized joint military exercise with Russia, that the new leaders are adopting bolder policies, fundamental change is not likely to take place in Hu Jintao's tenure, because Hu Jintao is a weak leader, possibly weaker than Jiang Zemin, who was phenomenally weaker than Deng Xiaoping. Although Hu Jintao might do tough things just to show that he is not a wimp, he would not dare to make big moves such as invading Taiwan.

The only reason for the Chinese leaders to invade Taiwan is to give themselves some breathing room to take care of internal problems. For China, it is a matter of when, not whether, social problems are going to cause large scale unrest. One of China's internal time bombs is the ever disappearing morality of the Chinese people, especially the young. In history, Jiang Zemin is going to be remembered as the leader who brought total corruption of morality to China. Under Jiang Zemin's watch, corrupt officials started to laugh at honest ones openly; prostitutes openly laugh at girls without money; and female college students dream about becoming some rich old men's mistresses. Other social problems include

---

12. The policy is known in Chinese as 韬光养晦, which means "emphasize on recovering". For instance, on August 19, 1991, Deng Xiaoping made it clear in an extended meeting of Politburo Standing Committee members in Beijing, including Yang Shangkun, Bo Yibo, and Song Renqiong, that the Chinese policy is "冷静观察，稳住阵脚，沉着应付，韬光养晦，善于守拙，绝不当头" (English translation: "Observe calmly; take a conservative stance; respond with cool head; emphasize on recovering; react only; and never lead any charges.")

the sexual imbalance of the newborns. In combination, as the rich begin to have multiple wives, and the boy-to-girl ratio reaches the level of 120:100, hundreds of millions of the Chinese people are not going to be able to find wives. That could trigger some serious social problems as the rich rapidly become richer and the poor remain poor.

For the international community, the best way to contain China's threat is to develop plans to handle the problems that the Chinese government itself is not going to be able to.

After MADly staring at each other for almost 50 years, the Soviet Union no longer exists. Russia, with all its problems, is one of America's strategic partners. At least so far, China displays its military power more for its internal propaganda purposes than in preparation of any imminent aggression. The challenge to the United States is from the Middle East in the form of terrorist attacks.

Since WWII, the economic development of the Middle East has been highly uneven because of oil. Those with oil have access to money and the West. They receive the best education in the West, invest in the West, and participate in the Western life as full partners, while those without oil are among the poorest in the world.

People living in poverty might cause no fuss to others as long as the intelligent ones have a way out, because poor people could not launch any real challenge to the rich without intelligent leadership. In the United States, generation after generation of poor people live in the inner city areas even when they typically live minutes away from prosperity because their intelligent sons and daughters always have a way to leave.

In modern Middle East, terrorists are led by intelligent and experienced leaders. Take Osama bin Laden for example. He, along with other mujahadins[13], was trained by the U.S. government, CIA to be more specific, to fight against the Soviet Union in Afghanistan. In the battle against the Soviet Union, they gained real battlefield experience. The defeat of the Soviet Union gave them confidence. It does not take a genius to figure out that the cheapest bomb delivery system is the religious fanatics who are willing to be suicide bombers in exchange for a pitiful sum of money. Osama bin Laden must have thought that he could defeat the United States just like that he had defeated the Soviet Union.

Prior to 9/11, unable to take out people like Osama bin Laden, the United States in fact had been a sitting duck. For instance, when Sudan finally decided to

---

13. The mujahadins are those who would die in a jihad, or holy war.

get rid of bin Laden, it offered to hand over bin Laden to the United States. Bill Clinton, thinking in legal terms that he did not have enough evidence to make a case against bin Laden, said no. With clear link between bin Laden and the 1993 attempt to bomb the World Trade Center in New York, CIA only tried to force Sudanese government to expel him. How could Bill Clinton refuse to take bin Laden? To bin Laden, the United States must have appeared to be, as Mao Zedong labeled it, a paper tiger.

His 1998 bombings of the United States embassies in Tanzania and Kenya and his 2000 attack on the U.S.S. Cole in Yemen did not create much response from the United States either. When literally everyone in the United States government knew that an attack on the U.S. mainland was coming, there was no proactive coherent strategy to stop it. In this sense, 9/11 was inevitable.

That was the problem facing the relatively new president George W. Bush who came to the White House at the beginning of 2001. One of the solutions was prepared by Paul Wolfwitz, his Deputy Secretary of Defense, a long time ago. Wolfwitz's idea was taking the battle to the enemy by invading Iraq. After the United States establishes a democratic and prosperous Iraq, the rest of the Middle Eastern nations would see the light and follow.

It is certainly a bold move, but compared to other alternatives, it has the best chance of solving the terrorist problem in the long run. Since it is impossible for the U.S. to conduct a MAD Cold War against the terrorists, the most relevant positive experience is the handling of Germany and Japan after WWII. Bush wanted to use that experience again in Iraq to uproot the Middle Eastern terrorist problems once and for all.

The terrorists reacted as expected by focusing their actions in Iraq. By keeping the American death toll growing, terrorists wanted to make Iraq another Vietnam for the U.S., hoping that the American people would force their government to withdraw. Both sides know that the key is whether the U.S. could restore order in Iraq. Once the order is restored in Iraqi, the U.S. would have a firm foothold in the Middle East, and the terrorists know that their days would be over. In fact, any direct attacks on the United States or Europe probably would do the terrorists a disservice because they would harden the resolve of the American and British people.

As long as the democratic process in Iraq is moving ahead, the United States is destined to win, because the Iraqi people will be tired of killing one day and cooperate with the authorities to get rid of the foreign terrorists. Before that happens, many Iraqis would still blame the U.S. for their problems, especially when the Americans are far from blameless. For instance, in order to reduce the number of American soldiers in Iraq, Pentagon is actively outsourcing military duties to private contractors. The best way to describe these private security contractors is that they are the modern day cowboys. In the process of protecting their clients, these private contractors, who put their lives on the line every day, often open fire against the terrorist suspects when innocent Iraqis were in the immediate proximity. If they wrongfully kill any Iraqis, there is no way for the Iraqis to redress the issue. In this sense, the war in Iraq is like the war in Vietnam, where lawlessness is fueling anti-American sentiment.

At the present time, the United States has difficulties breaking into the terrorist organizations and taking out its leadership, while the terrorist organizations are quite successful infiltrating the Iraqi security forces, which is trained and armed by the United States.

In conclusion, although the situation in Iraq could still go either way, the steadfast and successful democratic progress is tilting the balance toward a U.S. victory, as the Iraqi people come to recognize that a U.S. victory is their victory; and a U.S. defeat is their defeat.

Also, since the terrorists have attacked the U.S. mainland on 9/11, it is unlikely that future presidents will withdraw troops and allow a terrorist victory, because they would know that, if Iraq falls into terrorists' hands, it would become the biggest terrorist base against the rest of the world. The U.S. mainland would be one of their primary targets.

The United States, in one way or another, would be in Iraq for a long time. The task of reforming Iraq is at least as difficult as reforming in Germany and Japan. Germany before WWII was a Western power. For Japan, since the Meiji Reform (1868), Western thoughts were widely introduced and adopted, which enabled Japan to develop the modern armed forces to invade much of Asia successfully.

In Iraq, however, the Iraqi people do not have such a strong "Western" experience. Everyday, they see American cowboys shooting at them, their democratic government siphoning away money that should be used to solve their daily problems, and its won police forces infiltrated by terrorists, quite thoroughly in some places.

Somehow, Iraqi people have to recognize that the American soldiers have brought them only an opportunity of a bright future, no more, no less. They have to figure out how to use the opportunity to establish their own post-Saddam society, knowing that a misstep here might send Iraq back into terror for generations.

American withdrawal from Vietnam was certainly a defeat for the U.S. , but it is by no means a victory for the Vietnamese people. After Americans left Vietnam, the next news coming out of Vietnam was its widespread internal persecutions and the so-called "boat people"—people who were persecuted by their own government and forced to sell everything they owned and leave Vietnam by taking small boats that were not sea-worthy. The news from Iraq after a premature American pullout could be just as ugly.

Global terrorism is neither an American problem nor a British problem. France and Germany are hit just as hard, but they want to be cute by disagreeing with the United States and staying on the sidelines. That is the luxury for the second-tier countries in the world. Interestingly, Britain, which was the superpower before the United States, stood by the U.S. because it understands the responsibilities as a member of the world community.

One may say that France and Germany are taking advantage of the United States. By denouncing the American invasion of Iraq, it does not have to bother with the task of defeating terrorism. If the United States wins, they get the benefit anyway; if the U.S. loses, they would not be alone as losers.

France is quite good at taking advantage of the U.S. When China was tired of spending all the money to buy Russian military equipment, it tried to get Western equipment so it could more effectively threaten Taiwan. France stepped up to do China's bidding by pushing NATO[14] to lift the ban and allow sale of weapons to China. For its trouble, China opened a French Cultural Center in Beijing as its way to thank the French government. This is a textbook case of Prisoner's Dilemma. Taiwan is nowhere near the United States or France. According to the Chinese law, if Taiwan declares independence, the Chinese government would be obligated to invade Taiwan. Such invasion would certainly cause massive contraction of the world economy, not to mention the task of defending Taiwan against the Chinese invasion, but that is in the future; someone else would do it. Selling weapons to China, however, would benefit France economy presently. Now, without Saddam Hussein as its customer, France wants to promote its economy the quick way, by selling arms to potential aggressors, and leave the task of containment to others, namely the U.S. , Japan, and Taiwan.

For people who are not directly hit by terrorists, terrorism could be viewed as a form of tax, composed of additional cost in security measures (e.g., more tech-

---

14.   The North Atlantic Treaty Organization

nologies and more security personnel) and the sharing of damages caused by terrorists (e.g., higher insurance premiums). On top of that, there is a mental premium as people have to be ready to be hit. With their policies, France and Germany are evading the tax on them, forcing the U.S. to pay their share.

Many think that a multilateral international organization could solve the common problems of the world. But by examining the records of the United Nations, the U.N. itself as a body has never been a player. When forces are used under U.N. flags, it would be used anyway without U.N. , just like the U.S. invasion of Iraq. If the U.N. had not authorized the use of forces in Korea or Kuwait, there should be no doubt in anyone's mind that the U.S. would have used forces any way. In fact, Harry Truman ordered the American forces to Korea first and then obtained the U.N. Security Council resolution approving the use of forces against North Korea. So, if the Soviet Union had not been going though its emotional spell and vetoed the resolution, the American GIs would be fighting in Korea anyway. To say that the Americans in Korea were U.N. troops is the equivalent of saying that the "Chinese Volunteers" that subsequently entered Korea to aid the North were truly volunteers.

One might argue that the First Persian Gulf War (1991) was the true expression of the world opinions when the American-led U.N. forces repelled Iraqi invaders from Kuwait, but nobody should doubt that, without the U.N. support, Bush Sr. would have gone anyway. The reason for Bush Sr. to go through the trouble of putting together the coalition, especially one that included some Middle Eastern nations, is to make the subsequent military operations easier. At first, people argue about the wisdom for Bush Sr. to go to the U.N. and put his reputation and that of the president of the United States on the line because it was not clear whether he would ultimately get the support, but he went through the diplomatic arm-wrestling and got the U.N. mandate. If he had failed at U.N., he would have fought an awkward war any way.

Even if we admit that U.N. had something to do with the start of that war, it certainly had nothing to do with the end of the war which was determined exclusively by the White House.

In the case of Bush Jr. , a true Texan cowboy, he did not even want to play the U.N. game but went to the U.N. General Assembly and delivered his automaton to the world that that the U.S. was going to invade Iraq with or without the U.N. support. In the end, without Bush giving "incentives" to the Security Council members to get their support, the U.N. did not support the war and Bush went anyway.

Initially, the U.N. was formed to solve critical international problems. In reality, in those critical moments, the powerful nations are going to act the way they wish, regardless the result of the committee vote either of the General Assembly or the Security Council. In the case of Bush Jr., he did not bother to go through the process of bribing Security Council members so they would vote against terrorism.

Uniting the weaker powers against the stronger is also a theory that looks good on paper but could not be put into action. In the Chinese *zhanguo* period (476 B.C.–221 B.C.), facing the invading Qin armies, many people tried to unite the rest of the nations against the common enemy. All efforts failed.

A quick look at the Middle East would reveal that Israel is but a tiny island in the vast ocean of Arab nations. Since the 1948 Arab-Israeli War, known to Israelis the War of Independence[15] and to Arabs the Catastrophe[16], Israeli-Palestinian conflicts have been a constant problem. In fact, if Arab nations could have been united in the effort to defeat Israel, the task would not have been difficult.

Initiatives conducted by skillful individuals have a better chance to work out. For instance, Otto von Bismarck (1815–1898), more than anyone else, was responsible for keeping Europe in peace for 20 years through his diplomatic efforts. For those who would argue that Bismarck's diplomatic power was gained through his successful wars, Josip Tito (1892–1980) kept Balkans together in peace from 1943 to 1980, through mostly his personal influence. Tito was so impressive that, when he visited abroad, separatists would take actions. As soon as he returned, they would stop. After Tito died, it was only a matter of time when a Slobodan Milosevic would come along and the situation would get out of hands. At first, the U.N. did not do anything to prevent the genocide, and only sent in troops after the situation was already out of control. In a way, the Balkan situation was like that of Germany under Bismarck. After the death of Bismarck, his Reich fell apart as Europe went to war.

Other so-called diplomatic moves are purely tactical military or political moves. For instance, the infamous peace treaty between Neville Chamberlain and Hitler was merely a sham for Hitler to buy time. Chamberlain's declaration that he had won peace for the world after signing the treaty with Hitler has been told as a joke from generation to generation.

---

15. Hebrew: מלחמת העצמאות
16. Arabic: النكبـة

When the United States needed a face-saving way to withdraw from Vietnam, Le Duc Tho signed the peace treaty with Henry Kissinger. Interestingly, that treaty is not considered as laughable as the Chamberlain-Hitler one. In fact, Kissinger and Le were awarded the 1973 Nobel Peace Prize for what they did for "peace".

The reason that game playing has little place in international affairs is that the superpowers typically do not yield to the pressures of others. Certainly there are situations when France would take advantage of the United States by opposing the war in Iraq or selling arms to China, but the U.S. would stop France when it has gone too far. France could take advantage of others only because the U.S. allows it to. In any case, no nation has become world power by taking irresponsible actions that benefit itself at the expense of the rest of the world.

By comparing Arab nations and NATO members, there are common problems, such as members (e.g., France and Germany) taking advantage of others. The difference is in the extent of such activities. At NATO, countries such as France and Germany would restrict itself to a reasonable degree in its exploitation of others. In Arab countries however, such exploitation goes much further that it damages the fundamental relations of the nations.

It is not easy to keep an alliance going. Dwight D. Eisenhower proved that during WWII when he spent most of his time and energy to keep the alliance together. One of the reasons that NATO is stronger than the League of Arab States is that NATO members, while exploiting others, could still see the reason that they are together in the first place. That is the reason France is having difficulties to start selling weapon to China, because other members see the danger and would not want to rush to sell weapons to China to earn a fast buck.

To look at this from another angle, if less powerful nations could do things rationally, they would become powerful. The standard of reasonableness is not high. For example, China, inarguably a dictatorship nation that does not grant its citizens freedom of speech, association, or practicing religion, has become one of the economic powers in the world since Deng Xiaoping allowed the people to make money in the early 1980s.

With every implementation of reasonableness, there would be resistance from the vested interests who have been taking unreasonable advantage of others. These vested interests are typically people in power and/or with influence. The success of reform to implement reasonableness depends on the balance of the power of the reformers who intent to make the society more reasonable and the conservatives who want to keep the status quo.

If the United States, Britain, and other members of the coalition could successfully uproot terrorism, the existing international trade infrastructure and modern communication technologies may push the world into another *zhanguo* period, when nations could focus on helping one another (e.g., trading consumer goods) rather than damaging one another (e.g., launching wars or trading arms).

In that sense, George W. Bush was right on the money when he sent American troops to Iraq, as it is the quickest way to eliminate terrorism and usher in a period of development that the world has never seen.

10

Concluding Remarks

You will know the truth, and the truth will set you free.

—John 8:32

According to the Game Theory, in interpersonal relations, those who set out to take advantage of others could benefit from those who want to improve the relation.

Assume we have a group of people who put interests of others above their own. One might think that this is a heavenly society, but such a societal structure is highly unstable. Sooner or later, a new comer or someone in the group would take advantage of others. Since everyone else wants to help, that person stands to gain at the expense of others. This is not going to last long because some other me-too persons would follow suit. Once the pendulum starts swinging, everyone would run for cover and focus on protecting their self-interests. The name of the game is how to take advantage of others. A new equilibrium point would be reached because cooperation is necessary to accomplish certain tasks. At this point, self-interests of all participating parties drive cooperative efforts. To Ayn Rand, this is the only kind of cooperation that a society should promote because it allows the expression of individuality.

The problem with this system is that, in a society that is completely free of intervention, more productive people would be in the position to exploit others, leading to an exploitation structure that a few exploit the rest. That is not a stable situation because the masses would want to topple the few. In the United States, the solution came in the form of FDR's new deal, when the government passed a variety of laws, such as anti-monopoly laws, labor laws, and minimum wage laws. These laws re-balanced the demands and supplies in the labor market, allowing labor to use these laws to leverage against the employers. The pendulum swung too far as unions started to make excessive requests.

One of the features of democracy is that the wheel turns extremely slowly. Take the United States for example. Presidential elections are held once very four years. Members of Congress face their constituencies in two or six years. Under such a system, it took people some 50 years to figure out the problems of big government, and put Ronald Reagan, who started preaching for smaller government since 1960s, into the White House, so he could initiate the two-decade economic boom, and force the collapse of the Soviet Union.

It remains to be seen how long people would wait before giving politicians the mandate to reform the educational system. In order for the politicians to have an upper hand against the teachers associations, education has to be the determining issue of the elections, which is difficult because economy and national security always take higher priority. Even if education is the top issue, there is no guarantee whatsoever that the reform-minded politicians would prevail over teachers' class struggle theories. The only good thing in educational reform is that the solutions, starting with the voucher system, are all there. The only work left is the implementation.

The same situation exists in family life, as the spouse who does not care about the relation stands to take advantage of the one who does. The only way to solve the problem is for both spouses to recognize that promoting their self-interests through the promotion of common interests is far more beneficial than promoting self-interests at the expense of the other. That is why it is so difficult for people with different background to live together happily, because their differences make it so much harder to identify the common approach. When most couples admit that they have a fundamental problem, the relation is often beyond repair because the established subconscious filters of both parties are geared to promote their self-interests by screwing the other spouse.

In workplace, we see two kinds of people. The first kind tries to get the work done to the best of their ability. The second kind focuses on how to do less work and use the energy to promote themselves. Facing an incompetent manager, the second kind normally wins, forcing the first kind to make the choice of either joining the bureaucrats or being squeezed out.

In politics, it is easy for a small group of people to take advantage of the whole population. The government gives them money to work on noble causes to benefit other people, e.g., the poor. They can and always do spend a portion of that money to protect their interests. On the contrary, the reformers who want to stop them have to make voters recognize the hypocrisy of those noble causes, and are at a competitive disadvantage because they have to spend money from other sources to get the attention of the voters. Furthermore, the beneficiaries of these projects always give some money back to the politicians in the form of campaign contributions, thus help the politicians keep their offices and keep supplying the special interests groups. That is the Game Theory reason for the existence of so many pork barrel projects and so few reform measures.

In international relations, since politicians are responsible only to its own citizens, there is less game to be played. Besides arms sales, the protection of environment is one of the issues that the Game Theory is most relevant, because polluters stand to gain economically. For instance, one nation could release significantly more carbon dioxide than the others, and therefore promotes the living standard of their own people.

Another game in the international affair is weapon development, which reduces the security and the living standard for all as weapons become more and more efficient. When one nation develops a weapon system threatening others, other nations are forced to develop their own. The mere effect of such development is an arms race that all nations have to waste money on it so they won't be blackmailed down the road. In the Cold War, the United States forced the Soviet Union to spend so much money on the weapon systems that ultimately collapsed the Soviet economy. If the two countries could come to some arrangement so they don't have to carry out the arms race, their people, especially the Soviet people, would suffer much less.

Another common form of game is played through the third party payer system, such as the educational system and the healthcare system, where the service providers are paid by the third party to provide services to the service receivers. In the educational system, with police and jail, the government forces everyone to pay teachers so they would provide services to the students. In the medical insurance field, insurance companies pay the physicians to take care of the insured.

In fact, the third party payer system is essentially a version of the same situation. In the medical insurance case, the patient pays certain amount of premium. When he is sick, he tends to get as much medical treatment as possible, necessary as well as unnecessary. In the end, since everyone tries to take advantage of others by asking for more services, the insurance companies have to raise premiums. HMO was insurance companies' solution. By transferring some of the risk to physicians, insurance companies hoped that physicians would not subscribe unnecessary treatment, at the risk of not subscribing necessary treatment.

The educational system has another layer of isolation where parents pay the government to pay teachers to educate their children, who might not care about the quality of the services. Since teachers get their money from the government, that uses police and jail to compel the public to pay up, they focus their attention on themselves and the government. First, teachers implement a tenure system under which they practically could not be fired. Second, teachers are paid by a fixed the pay scale that makes their salary entirely dependent upon their degree and their years of service as teachers. Their performance is not factored into the formula. This measure effectively stops anyone from entering teaching profession at mid-career. Third, they use the molding method to teach rather than the Montessori Method. Fourth, they force all teachers to pay teachers associations that would campaign to stop any reform. At the same time, they lobby the parents that all evils of the educational system come from the lack of funding, so the parents ought to push the government to increase educational funding. So far, teachers associations have been so successful that all politicians are afraid of them.

Since medical insurance operations have a private side as companies or the insured are willing to pay only up to a certain level, and patients always demand certain level of services, there is a limit for the maximum premium and minimum services. When PPO cost finally went beyond companies' ability to pay, the insurance industry was forced to reform by providing HMO.

In the educational system, teachers simply have to make the parents think that they are doing a good job, which is different from actually doing a good job. Their argument is that all problems in the system are caused by government's failure to pay them sufficient money. Since the educational system misinforms the parents or simply blocks the information regarding alternative theories of education such as the Montessori Method, the public is largely ignorant. Also, since those who disagree with the educational system typically could afford to send their children to alternative schools such as the Montessori schools, or live in the area with good public schools, or home-school their children, we don't see people bother to put up the vain effort to reform the public educational system. That is why reformers could never rally enough support to make the necessary reforms.

George W. Bush, who favored school vouchers, abandoned that effort after seeing the power of the teachers associations. In California, teachers put on around-the-year advertising campaigns against Arnold Schwarzenegger in response to his effort to weaken the power of teachers' organizations and caused Schwarzenegger's decline in popularity.

So, how can a society stop people like teachers who take advantages of the rest of the society?

Ayn Rand had an answer. "My philosophy, in essence," she declared, "is the concept of man as a heroic being, with his own happiness as the moral purpose of his life, with productive achievement as his noblest activity, and reason as his only absolute."[1] Rand called this objectivism.

In other words, an objectivistic society does not allow anyone to take advantage of others. In Rand's world, nobody sacrifices for others. For example, in an objectivistic educational system, teachers are paid according to what they have done to students, not the number of years that they have been teaching.

The path to such a heroic (i.e., objectivistic) system is actually quite simple: People should be paid reasonably, i.e., according to what they do.

First, understanding is the basis for people to act reasonably. Many factors in this world, such as our biological-biochemical design and our subconscious filters, cause shortcomings in our physical and psychological system. With those shortcomings, some fools could believe that piloting planes into the World Trade Center and killing innocent people would bring them to heaven or solve the problems of the world.

Thinkers go against their natural tendencies by using their emotions to drive their efforts to understand. In fact, all thinkers are passionate people, because they need the élan for the energy to keep plowing in the dark and counter the seemingly hopelessness.

In corporations, it is simply impossible for executives to specialize in all aspects of their companies (i.e. sales, marketing, finance, production, research and development, etc.), but they need to understand enough of each aspect to make good general policy decisions. That requires the ability to understand abstractions directly without the supporting details, a tall order for any individual. A shining example of such success is Jack Welch, who owed much of his success to his efforts of understanding GE's myriad of businesses. When he ran into situations that he did not understand, he simply traveled to the business unit and asked the responsible people to explain it to him, which became a learning process for him and a test for the managers. Most likely, those who failed to explain their tasks clearly to Welch did not know what they were doing and thus were unfit to lead. Through heavy traveling and the purposeful efforts to understand, Welch had a comfortable comprehension of the whole spectrum of GE's busi-

---

1.　Ayn Rand, Appendix to *Atlas Shrugged*

nesses and proved himself a masterful grand strategist. Under his leadership, Welch increased the profitability of individual business units far more than what he, in the form of GE's corporate overhead, cost each business unit.

According to my experience, knowing what questions to ask about an unfamiliar subject demonstrates a person's ability to understand abstractions. Often, the challenge is not the lack of information but the inability to make sense of all the details, which was Jimmy Carter's problem. If the top management could not understand what is going on in different business units, bureaucrats, rather than innovators, would rule.

Since most of us would rather allow unchecked blind emotions to make decisions for us, indoctrination is often the choice method of persuasion instead of education. For instance, after successful indoctrination, Germans helped Hitler cleanse Jews; the Chinese helped Mao Zedong eliminate his political enemies during the Cultural Revolution; the Russians helped Stalin carry out his brutal rule; the Americans helped Joseph McCarthy persecute suspect communists; Arab fools helped Osama bin Laden kill innocent people; and the public, believing in Marxist class struggle theories, voted against school voucher propositions.

Once indoctrination is done successfully, it is almost impossible to change the minds of those people again. Keynesianism, communism, and other misguided theories could last for a generation because once people are convinced that those theories are the best way for the society, they would refuse to visit the issue again. One has to wait for the next generation to discover the falsehood, establish new consensus, and reform.

Many people have told me that preschool education is not important, children do not learn before they go to elementary schools. It is true enough that children do not learn certain subjects until they go to elementary schools, but they get their temperament, their general view of the world, their way to handle problems, and their communication skills, from the day they are born. Many Chinese immigrants, who want to focus their energy exclusively on their career, send their newborn children to their parents or siblings in China for upbringing, and take them back when they are about to go to school. In almost every single case, the change from the Chinese culture to the American culture confuses the children so much that few could make a clean transformation.

Since the educational system does not educate people for what they are (like the Montessori schools) but tries to mold them according to school's pre-existing curricula and uses incentive such as pride and jealousness (i.e., grade point average or ranking) instead of the fun of proactive "understanding", students are pushed to be slaves rather than masters.

This problem is extremely bad where children do not have alternatives, such as in the inner city areas, where few have witnessed independent studying and academic curiosity. On the contrary, children of upper and middle class families could often see their parents demonstrating curiosity, analytical skills, and pleasure of public discourse.

Second, we need to put the understanding into practice with leadership skills and malcontent. If understanding is the fight against our own latencies, putting ideas into practice involves changing the latencies of others, which must overcome, among other things, poor biological-biochemical designs, subconscious filters, and Prisoner's Dilemmas. In an organizational setting, for instance, if a person pushes for change, all bureaucrats would mark the reformer as public enemy number one, and move in coordination to destroy him viciously in the true spirit of self-preservation. In current business environment, many people are promoted to positions beyond their abilities and quickly become reactionaries. All they want to do is to drift with the trend.

Standing up against the trend could be a risky undertaking. In China, during the Cultural Revolution, with few exceptions, most people who recognized the stupidities of the Communist Party and Mao Zedong chose to remain silent, allowing Mao Zedong to use the Red Guards to destroy the existing Chinese official system and eliminate the few who dared to open their mouths. I had the privilege in China to know some of these thinkers. Out of boredom or habit, they kept on figuring things out while consciously restricting themselves from any attempts to display their understandings publicly. Although they largely won their peace of mind, the nation missed the opportunities to use their talents. Throughout China, those who recognized the true nature of the Cultural Revolution were an extreme minority. The overwhelming majority participated in the Cultural Revolution and was used by Mao Zedong to drive his oppositions out of offices. After Mao Zedong finished using the young Red Guards, for example, he sent them to the countryside to be "reeducated" to avoid these confident youth from turning on him. The generation of youth who grew up during the Cultural Revolution ended up being known as the wasted generation.

The U.S. is lucky in this regards because thinkers, especially the founding fathers, recognized the importance of free exchange of ideas. They got together and risked their lives by declaring independence from Britain to build, according to their understandings, a better society in North America. Thomas Jefferson was one of those thinkers who steadfastly pushed for the important issues, such as freedom of speech, the separation of church and state, the emphasis on citizen's rights rather than that of the government, the abolition of slavery, an educational system that empowered the students rather than the teachers, etc. It is the first time in history that those in power went out of their way to reduce the power of government. Although Jefferson did not solve all those problems, such as that of slavery and education, history has demonstrated his wisdom and proved that those problems that he failed to solve are tough ones. The American society is still struggling with the racial problems more than a century after the abolition of slavery. The educational system is showing no sign of any imminent reform.

Best people follow true leaders. In Jefferson's case, James Madison and James Monroe worked with him to advance their common goals. One may say that without Jefferson and his lieutenants, the United States could not have been what it is today.

Recently, technological advances and various attempts to reach regional and global free trade agreements have made the world a much fairer place. American workers have to compete against people working in remote China township enterprises earning pennies a day. The only advantage that the American workers have over their Chinese competitors for the sales of goods in the United States is the shipment cost, which is amazingly low because of the economy of scale.

As far as the United States is concerned, competition on the basis of labor cost is a losing battle. The only way for the United States to keep its current position is through leading the world in breaking new grounds. The development of high tech equipment illustrates the dynamics of such change. Those who use technologies are going to be paid less and less because technological advances have been consistently reducing the need of skills, thus increasing number of people would be qualified to do the work; those who develop technologies, however, would be paid more and more because people throughout the world would be able to use the developed technologies.

The nasty part of the 2000 economic slowdown is that it hit the creative part of the economy the hardest, forcing many creative workers inside the U.S. into less creative jobs, which was at best underutilization or waste, and at worst, forfeiting the future of the United States. In a shrinking world, the margin for error is becoming smaller and smaller. Companies such as Microsoft and Oracle have established their research and development centers in India and China. If the American financial markets keep suffocating high-tech U.S. sectors, other nations might create the next new industry and earn the creative premium instead.

There are many steps that the government could take to stimulate the U.S. creative sector.

First, the government could force companies to be transparent. For instance, SEC could forbid the "generally accepted" nonsense and adopt uniform accounting principles. Companies should bear the burden to explain to the public why the uniform accounting principle does not do justice to their businesses. The difficulty of this step is, of course, the unwillingness of the finance professional to give up the sexy part of their *raison d'être,* and the ineffectiveness of the public influence.

Second, tax cut is the most obvious move to encourage people to take risks in new technologies. For instance, Reagan tax cut unleashed waves of investment, which ultimately led to the information technologies revolution, raising the living standard of the rich as well as the poor. The Democratic Party is using class struggle theory to stop the Bush tax cut. The difficulty of this step is that the majority, resentful of the rich, are more ready to stand up and force the government to take back its tax cut than the rich to stand up and openly announce that they urgently need more money to take the necessary risks.

In a democracy, the people decide the future of their nation. If the American people fail to have the government encourage the innovative segment of the society to take risks and allow another nation to lead the next round of revolution, the people only have themselves to blame. In fact, the innovative elite would figure out a way to take advantage of the new development any way, for instance, by moving abroad, because the nation that leads the next technological revolution would be hungry for talents. The people who are left behind are the lower and middle class people.

Understanding, or "knowing thyself" as Thales put it, is important; taking action with the understanding is equally important, because understanding without taking action is pointless. There is no question that Zhou Enlai, the late premier of China, understood the true nature of Mao Zedong and the Cultural Revolution, as he was regarded by many, including Richard Nixon and Gerald Ford, as the greatest politician ever. But, in the harsh political environment of the Cultural Revolution, Zhou Enlai often carried out Mao Zedong's dirty deeds, which made him a tragic figure in the voluminous annals of the Chinese history. Deng Xiaoping later commented about the role that Zhou Enlai played in the Cultural Revolution: Without Zhou Enlai, China would have suffered a lot more during the Cultural Revolution; but with him, Mao Zedong was able to carry on his Cultural Revolution for much longer. If Zhou Enlai had dared to take action, whether or not he had prevailed, he would have been remembered as a hero.

Think (therefore understand) and act (therefore make improvement) go hand-in-hand in the battle against lies, just as Chinese *qigong* makes mental training and physical exercise two inseparable aspects of the exercise.

Index

978-0-595-38602-4
0-595-38602-4

www.ingramcontent.com/pod-product-compliance
Lightning Source LLC
Chambersburg PA
CBHW020427290526
45785CB00002B/730